Rich Tales From Early California

Alton Pryor

Rich Tales From Early California

Alton Pryor

Stagecoach Publishing
5360 Campcreek Loop
Roseville, CA 95747
(916) 771-8166
stagecoach@surewest.net
www.stagecoachpublishing.com

Rich Tales From Early California

Library of Congress
Control Number: 2008903196

ISBN: 0-9660053-7-6

History is not dead;
It's not even past.

William Faulkner

The Island of California

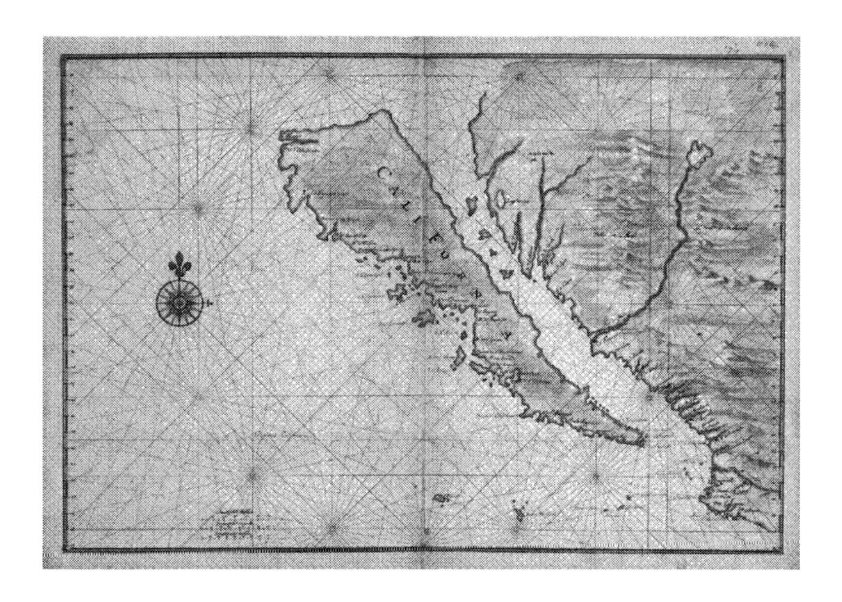

Early explorers thought California was an island. (Google Images)

Early in the sixteenth century, Spanish writer Garci Rodriguez Ordonez de Montalvo published a book called Las Sergas de Esplandian (The Exploits of Esplandian). One of the characters in this fantasy was Calafia, the queen of California, "more beautiful than all the rest."

Montalvo described this mythical California as an island inhabited solely by black women who lived "in the manner of Amazons."

Historians assume that Montalvo's novel was

known to the Spanish explorers who first sailed along the coast of Baja California peninsula in the early 1500s.

Apparently the explorers named the peninsula "California" after the mythical island in the novel. Hernán Cortés, the conqueror of the Aztec empire, reported in 1524 that he expected to find an island of Amazons along the Montalvo's novel includes these words:

"Know ye that on the right hand of the Indies there is an island called California, very near the Terrestrial Paradise and inhabited by black women without a single man among them and living in the manner of Amazons. Their island is one of the most rugged in the world with bold rocks and crags.

California was depicted on maps as an island for more than 100 years, even after Father Kino established its penisularity about 1705.

Table of Contents

Chapter 1

California: Before Statehood

California stretches its coastline for 1,264 miles as it winds, twists and turns to form its beaches and harbors.

If the Mayflower had landed on California's Pacific coast, instead of the eastern seaboard, California most probably would have been cut up into several small states, similar to the New England region.

California is indeed an unusual state. It contains both the lowest point and the highest point in the continental U.S. It is 282 feet below sea level at Badwater, Death Valley, and 14,495 feet above sea level at Mt. Whitney.

The earliest Californians to arrive were not the Spanish. They were the adventurist Asians who crossed the Bering Straits to Alaska thousands of years ago. Then, a now-gone land bridge made such travel easier.

These early arrivals spread out to settle North and South America. They are the same people that the Europeans dubbed "Indians" when they first arrived in this hemisphere.

A tiny portion of California's twelve hundred mile coastline can be seen in this photo.
(State of California Photo)

Because the area was isolated by giant mountain ranges, the native peoples, in what is now known as California, were isolated. They were isolated from the cultures of Mexico and from the Great Plains tribes as well.

Some say as many as 135 distinct dialects were spoken across the west.

The mountains that separated the various cultures served as a barrier to tribal warfare. The California tribes and clans enjoyed a comparatively peaceful life.

Hernando Cortez ventured to Baja California in the 1530s, but it wasn't until Juan Rodriguez Cabrillo made an expedition to Alta California in

1542 that the Spanish became interested. Cabrillo made landings as far north as today's Santa Barbara, laying claim to the coastal regions.

Still, Spain made no effort to colonize the territory until another two hundred years passed.

Even then, colonization was limited to the Baja region. Baja California became the northwest limit of Spanish colonization. Attempts to settle the area and bring native tribes to Christianity were half-hearted.

Settlement came through a combination of military forts or presidios, and mission churches led by Father Junipero Serra. By the end of the Spanish colonial period Alta California had three more presidios (at Monterey, San Francisco, and Santa Barbara). But under Father Serra's guidance, there were 21 missions.

Small towns (pueblos) also sprang up. The earliest of these were associated with the missions and presidios, but in 1777, an independent civil pueblo was created at San Jose.

The pueblo was governed by an alcalde (a combination judge-mayor in today's vernacular).

When the first Europeans came to California, it is estimated there were about 300,000 natives. Sixty-five years later, because of their exposure to the Europeans and their diseases, the population was reduced to 150,000.

The natives had little or no resistance to the European diseases, and thousands died in epidemics. Contributing to this was the harsh living conditions at the missions.

In 1816, Ukrainian-born expedition artist Louis Choris (1795-1828) produced the earliest and best drawings of California native people. Here is his depiction of the Monterey Presidio.

(Google Images)

Infant mortality and death rates among children soared.

It was more than 150 years after Sebastian Vizcaino had discovered Monterey Bay that Spain attempted to cement control of the region. There were rumblings of interest from other countries who might want the area.

Frederick Beechey (1796-1856), a British naval officer, led a scientific expedition to the Pacific during which he visited California in 1826. In a book he published about his trip are some of the best early drawings of the northern California missions. (Google Images)

Spain's King Charles sent Jose de Galvez to Mexico City as his special representative, or *visitor-general.* Galvez was variously described as energetic, efficient, and far-sighted on one hand, and mean, jealous, crafty, superstitious and ridiculously vain on the other.

From his Mexican seat of power, Galvez dispatched two vessels to transport soldiers and supplies to the port of Monterey. At the same time, an overland expedition was dispatched from the Spanish missions of Lower California, aiming for the same destination.

In charge of this overland expedition was Don Gaspar de Portola, and Fray Junipero Serra,

Father President of the Missions. A few days after reaching San Diego, Portola recognized the San Diego port as a royal presidio.

Historians have described the area as being in a forlorn and sorry state, with only a few brush huts in the depths of the wilderness in which resided a handful of scurvy-ridden men, surrounded by none too friendly savages.

Spain's King Charles III, a vigorous and able statesman, ordered Don Gaspar de Portola to lead an expedition to develop an overland trail from San Diego in search of Vizcaino's Monterey. Father Francisco Gomez and Father Juan Crespi, who kept a descriptive journal of the trip, accompanied him.

As Portola and his companions marched across the fertile plains and valleys near the coast, they made careful notes of the most desirable locations for settlements and missions. Every place of importance was given a name.

Ten days out of San Diego, the party felt a series of severe earthquakes, resulting in Father Crespi calling one stream, "the River of the Sweet Name of Jesus of the Earthquakes".

The leather-jacketed soldiers on the mission simply called the river the Santa Ana.

The expedition traveled through an Indian village whose inhabitants were skillful at carving wooden canoes. The explorers named the place Carpentaria. Later, a soldier is said to have killed a sea gull where the trail turned from the coast inland to the Santa Inez Valley. They named that pass Gaviota. The country through which the Spaniards traveled contained populations of friendly Indians.

The Indians were divided into many small tribes or clans, each living in its own village and speaking its own dialect. Unlike North American Indians who knew at least the rudiments of agriculture, growing such things as corn, beans, and melons, the California Indians raised no crops of any kind.

From San Diego to the foot of the Santa Lucia Mountains, just beyond San Luis Obispo, the Portola expedition found an easy trail.

When the last of the company crossed the mountains, they followed a course along the Salinas River to the sea. Excitement quickened when they sighted a point of land with a forest of pines and a bay. The expedition was sure it had found the long lost port of Monterey discovered by Vizcaino.

The more the explorers examined the bay, however, the less it resembled the descriptions left by Vizcaino and Father Ascension, who had accompanied him.

They decided they would have to renew their search for Monterey. With supplies dangerously low, they trudged onward, coming to the present site of Watsonville, Point Reyes, and the Farallones. Examining their charts, they now realized they had overshot the port of Monterey.

Portola ordered the expedition to give up the search and return to San Diego. The half-starved men were forced to eat some of their worn-out pack animals on the return trip to keep alive.

After a brief rest, and loaded with new supplies, they set out again in search of Monterey. They reached the Salinas Valley without serious incident. On careful examination, they soon convinced themselves their first sighting truly had been the bay of Monterey behind the point of pines.

Portola quickly took steps to occupy the harbor, which came to be known as "The Spanish Heart of California".

Historians recognize Portola as the first Governor of Alta California. In 1775, the King of Spain named Monterey the Capital of California.

Chapter 2

The Ship of Gold

The coins retrieved from the sunken treasure were found in near-perfect condition.
(Google Images)

On August 20, 1857, the S.S. Sonora sailed from San Francisco carrying 578 passengers and a gold shipment valued at $1.6 million. The gold was in all forms—dust, nuggets, coins and ingots, and represented one of the most important sagas in Gold Rush history.

The S.S. Central America was so-battered by a fierce hurricane that its cargo and 425 passengers were lost. (Google Images)

This valuable cargo and its passengers, were loaded on a narrow-gage railroad from the Pacific Ocean side in Panama and transferred to the United States Mail Steamship S.S. Central America on the Atlantic Ocean side for the long trip to New York.

Little did the passengers suspect they were on the last voyage of the S.S. Central America. After four days of sailing in calm seas, the ship dropped anchor in Havana Harbor to take on more coal and provisions.

Then on that tragic day in September of 1857, the 272-foot long side-wheel steamship S.S.

Central America was battered by a fierce hurricane off the coast of the Carolinas.

The wind was so strong that one passenger asked the ship's captain, Commander William Lewis Herndon, about shipwrecks. "If she goes down, I go under her keel," replied Herndon.

By morning, the weather had worsened. As a squall line approached, the passengers were forced to beat a hasty retreat below decks. By evening, the Central America was rolling in deep swells and many of the passengers in the cramped quarters below deck were in dire misery from seasickness.

By Friday, September 11, the Central America was taking on water and beginning to list. Commander Herndon had the ensign hoisted upside down to indicate the ship was in distress.

The brig *Marine* came upon the Central America about noon on September 12, 1857. Captain Herndon realized his ship was doomed. He loaded women and children into lifeboats and crewmen rowed them nearly three miles across stormy seas to the safety of the *Marine*.

Herndon, realizing his ship could not last the night, donned his full-dress uniform and climbed atop the paddlewheel. His last act was to fire off a set of rockets to indicate the ship was sinking fast.

The men aboard scrambled for life preservers, but the enormous suction of the sinking ship pulled many of them below. Many others who survived the pull of the sinking ship later drowned in the storm-driven waves.

Soon after midnight, the storm abated.

The Norwegian ship, *Ellen*, arrived on the scene and pulled some 50 men to safety.

The S.S. Central America took its $1.6 million in gold cargo and 425 passengers to the bottom of the Atlantic.

The wreck of the S.S. Central America was worst peacetime maritime disaster on record. The steamship was loaded with tons of California gold bars and a treasure chest filled with $20 Liberty gold coins dated 1857. These coins were newly minted from the San Francisco Mint. They would lie at the bottom of the Atlantic for 131 years.

The financial fallout from the sinking of the S.S. Central America and her cargo sparked a financial crisis of major proportions. The U.S. was in a recession during most of the 1850s, and the recession grew worse in August 1857 when the Ohio Life Insurance and Trust Company failed, leaving enormous debts.

Banks that had loaned money to Ohio Life Insurance and Trust found themselves overextended. Depositors demanded payment in gold from banks. This caused a domino effect. Bankers hoped the expected gold shipment aboard the S.S. Central America would ease the economic pressure.

With news of the shipwreck, the Panic of 1857 took hold, ruining many men and businesses. If the loss of such an enormous amount of gold, believed to be approximately three tons, was a drag on the economy, it was also a tempting prize for fortune hunters.

One of the first to seek the prize was a Brutus de Villeroi, an American citizen of French birth. He proposed finding the treasure with a submarine, which he had invented.

Atlantic Mutual Insurance Company, which had covered part of the losses aboard the S.S. Central America, readily agreed to give him a chance. His attempts ended in failure.

Marine biologist Thomas G. Thompson formed the Columbus-America Discovery Group in 1986 to locate the shipwreck. The 161 investors in the project raised more than $10 million.

Thompson would use a remarkable robotic recovery vessel, aptly named "*Nemo*". This vessel weighed some six tons and looked something like a cardboard box to which random bits and pieces of scrap metal and electronics were glued.

Nemo was tethered by more than two and a half miles of cable to a refurbished icebreaker called the Arctic Discoverer.

The robot utilized three-dimensional video imaging and carried an array of lights, lobster-like arms, and a vacuum. It could recover objects from the inky depths more than a mile and a half below the ocean's surface.

Marine biologists marveled at the photographs the robot took of the debris field—passengers' trunks, the ship's side-wheel and bell, which identified the ship as the S.S. Central America.

In his book, "America's Lost Treasure," biologist Thompson said the first gold ingots were spotted in October of 1988.

The robot Nemo was tethered by two-and-a-half miles of cable to the icebreaker Arctic Discoverer. (Google Images)

"Suddenly, the same monitors that had revealed nothing but colorless ocean terrain for weeks now appeared to be painted a brilliant gold.

These weren't bricks, but gold ingots everywhere, stacked like brownies, stacked like loaves of bread—spectacular gold bridges of gold ingots piled on top of timbers and spread over the ocean floor."

Thompson said that amidst the rotted wood, scattered gold dust, and coins, the Gold Rush bars lay toppled like dominos, some glinting brilliantly in the glare of Nemo's lights, and others lay like petrified wood. The rust streams from the deteriorating iron of the ship toned some of the bars.

It was the great depth to which the S.S. Central America had sunk that helped to preserve the precious treasure. At some 8,500 feet the temperatures of the ocean are frigid and the current nonexistent.

The soft surfaces of the gold were not etched by a flow of salt water or sediment, and the objects remained exactly where they fell. Columns of gold coins remained erect as the wooden boxes around them rotted. Piles of gold dust lay where once there had been a bag containing them.

Recovery of the treasure required all of Nemo's talents. Its grappling arms were required to lift gold bars weighing up to 62 pounds, including on ingot that was dubbed "*Eureka*" that weighed nearly 80 pounds.

The robot had to cover the stacks of coins with silicone rubber to transport them to the surface. It had to delicately place suction cups to retrieve the tiny flakes of gold that lay as though they had been freshly panned from the waters of a California river.

After the successful recovery, Thompson and his group faced a decade of litigation to keep the historic find. Eventually, courts awarded 92 percent of the treasure to Thompson.

The Gold Cargo of the S.S. Central America

The ship carried more than three tons of gold. (Google Images)

• 5,200 recently minted $20-denomination ("Double Eagle") gold pieces produced in 1857 at the San Francisco Mint.

• Privately made gold coins and ingots produced by such historic, government-supervised San Francisco Gold Rush era assayers as Blake & Co.; Kellogg & Humbert; Wass Molitor & Co.; and Harris, Marchand & Co.

• The largest and most valuable ingot recovered is an astonishing gold brick weighing 933 ounces, or nearly 80 pounds, made by Kellogg & Humbert.

The remainder went to Insurance Companies. The treasure was later sold to the California Gold Marketing Group, an organization of private investors.

The magnificent "Eureka" gold bar was part of a 16-month traveling exhibit that included $20 million worth of gold items recovered from the shipwreck.

In November 2001, the 933-ounce brick Eureka was sold for $8 million, making it the most expensive single collectible money item in history.

The value of the gold ingot was increased because of its dramatic history. An authority on private coin collections said it was not only the size of the ingot, but its links with the most romantic eras in American history that enhanced its value.

Chapter 3

Lillie Coit

Lillie Coit
(Google Images)

Lillie Hitchcock, at the age of eight, became trapped when fire raged through a building she and two other youngsters were exploring. As she stood in the midst of a ring of flames, above her, John Boynton, a substitute on San Francisco's Knickerbocker Number Five fire company hacked a hole through the roof.

Lowering himself on a rope, Boynton carried Lillie on his back while clambering hand-over-hand back up the rope to safety. The other youngsters perished in the fire. The date was December 23, 1851.

From then on, Lillie's affection for Knickerbocker No. 5 continued to grow.

At age fifteen, the fire company had a short staff on the ropes as it raced to a fire on Telegraph Hill. Because of the shortage of manpower, the engine was falling behind. It would have been humiliating to the firemen if Manhattan No. 2 or Howard No. 3 beat Knickerbocker to the fire. It was then that Lillie, on her way home from school, took action.

Lillie tossed her books to the sidewalk and dashed to a vacant place on the rope, at the same time, crying to the bystanders, "Come on, you men! Everybody pull and we'll beat 'em!"

And the bystanders did come and pull and Knickerbocker No. 5 was hurled up the slope and put first water on the fire.

From that day on, Lillie caught the spirit of the Volunteer Firemen, and they in turn responded. There was never a gala parade in which Lillie was not seen atop Knickerbocker No. 5. She was, literally, the patroness of all the firemen of her city.

Lillie was always something of a "tomboy". As a child, she romped in short frocks and was fascinated by the red shirt and warlike helmets worn by firemen. She gloried in the excitement of a big blaze.

While still in her teens, Lillie rushed to the scene of every fire when she heard the fire bell toll its alarms. She came to be regarded as a mascot by the firemen.

On October 3, 1863, Lillie was elected an honorary member of the Knickerbocker Company, and always regarded that honor as the proudest of her life. She wore the numeral and the gold badge the firemen had presented her with all her costumes.

Masculinely dressed, Lillie would leave whatever she was doing to attend a fire. Once she left a wedding party in which she was a bridesmaid.

The wealthy Hitchcocks, from whom Lilly inherited her wealth, were considered valued members of San Francisco Society, and her parents, especially her mother, frequently agonized over the actions of Lillie.

When Lillie's father, Dr. Charles Hitchcock heard about Lillie driving a team of horses at their Calistoga summer home, he didn't try to stop her. Instead, he hired Colonel Clark Foss, a noted stagecoach driver, to give her lessons.

According to one account, Lillie would often drive groups of her suitors, usually at breakneck speed to the White Sulphur Springs Hotel. Then, often as not, she beat the young men at poker while smoking cigars and helping polish off a bottle of bourbon.

Howard Coit first saw Lillie when she was riding Knickerbocker No. 5 back from a fire. "I was surprised," he said later, "...that she was incandescent rather than beautiful."

When Lillie sighted Coit, it was said to be love at first sight. They eloped in 1869, angering Lillie's mother who felt the young stockbroker not good enough for her daughter.Coit died in 1885, but he and Lillie had already been separated for five years. Their marriage had been fraught with suspicion and jealousy.

In 1904, it is reported that an assassin bent on killing her broke into her room while she was entertaining a Major McClurg. The major boldly defended her and subdued the assassin, but McClurg later died. The assassin, ruled insane by the courts, was assigned to a padded cell.

Lillie was so shaken by the event that she moved to Paris, where she lived for 20 years. It was not until the assassin died that Lillie returned to her beloved San Francisco.

When Lillie Coit died in San Francisco July 22, 1929, at the age of 86, she left one-third of her fortune to the city "to be expended in an appropriate manner for the purpose of adding to the beauty of the city which I have always loved."

The executors of her will, several years after her death, decided to erect a memorial tower in her honor and also as a memorial tribute to San Francisco's firemen.

Coit Tower, with its top shaped like a fire hose.

(Google Images)

This novel 180-foot cylindrical tower, shaped like a fire-nozzle, stands atop Telegraph Hill. A family mausoleum holds the remains of Lillie (she was cremated). Beside the niche where her ashes are stored can be seen a khaki fire jacket, a coiled fire hose, and a brass fire hose nozzle.

Chapter 4

Jedediah Smith, Mountain Man

Jedediah in the Badlands by, Harvey Dunn. (Google Images)

Jedediah Smith wanted to be the first to view a country on which a white man's eyes had never gazed.

In his lifetime, Smith would travel more extensively in unknown territory than any other single mountain man.

On his second expedition, Smith was attacked by a grizzly bear. The bear came out of a thicket, mauling him and literally ripped his scalp from his head. With the scalp hanging on to his head by an ear, Smith instructed Jim Clyman to sew it back on.

When Clyman said he didn't think he could do anything with the mountain man's severed ear, Smith insisted that he try.

"I put my needle sticking it through and through and over and over laying the lacerated parts together as nice as I could with my hands," Clyman wrote.

After two weeks of rest, Smith resumed his duty as captain of the party.

Smith kept a diary of his crossing of the Great Salt Lake Desert.

"At one point, we were obliged to stop under the shade of a small cedar," he wrote. "We dug holes in the sand and laid down in them for the purpose of cooling our heated bodies."

When Smith spotted several turtle doves, the sight heartened him, as he had never known doves to travel more than two or three miles from water. He spent an hour looking for water, without success.

The next day, Robert Evans laid down in the shade of a small cedar, unable to travel further. "We left him and proceeded onward in hopes of finding water in time to return to save his life," Smith recorded in his diary.

After traveling three miles, the party arrived at the foot of a mountain and joyfully found water. Smith wrote, "Goble plunged into it at once, and I could hardly wait to bath my burning forehead before I was pouring it down regardless of the consequences."

A grizzly tore the scalp from the head of Jedediah Smith He instructed and assistant to sew it back.
(Google Images)

In his journal, Smith said before arriving at the spring, he had seen two Indians headed in the direction the party had left Evans. Smith took a small kettle of water and some meat with him and found Evans was still safe.

While he was scarcely able to speak, Evans downed the water, which Smith said was at least four to five quarts. It revived him and he was able to accompany the mountain man to the spring.

Tall and silent, Smith never used tobacco or profanity. He had been reared a Methodist and was a devout Christian. When he encountered hardship or peril, such as his encounter with the grizzly, he resorted to Scripture for strength.

On his 1826 expedition, Smith entered California's San Bernardino Valley to become the first American to cross the southwestern part of the American continent.

Smith returned to California in 1828 with a company of 18 men by the same southern route he had used in 1826. This time, however, Mojave Indians attacked him. The Indians had been friendly two years earlier, but later outrages by white men sent them on the warpath.

Smith lost 10 men in the assault, which represented more than half of his company. He also lost most of his supplies and equipment. Smith and his men continued on and arrived at Mission San Gabriel in a ragged and half-starved condition.

Instead of greeting the party, the mission fathers clapped Smith and his men in the "calabozo" and then sent them in chains to Governor Jose Maria Echeandia in San Diego, who had blocked Smith's travel plans in 1826. Smith had defied the Governor's order and Echeandia was not happy to see him this time.

He incarcerated Smith and his men in appalling conditions. Finally, at the urging of a former English sea captain, and the threats of the American consul, Echeandia freed the party, giving them another exit visa from the province.

Smith was not only the first American to travel by land to California, but also the first to cross the Great Basin and the first (in early 1828) to reach Oregon by going up the great central valley of California.

It was Jedediah Smith who first named Mount Lassen "Mount Saint Joseph." The mountain bore the name of Mount Joseph for a generation.

Smith was killed in 1831 while leading a wagon train west on the Santa Fe Trail. Near Cimarron, Smith struck out on his own in an attempt to locate fresh water, and was ambushed by a band of Comanche Indians.

With two six-shooters blazing, Smith held the Comanches at bay until his horse spooked and whirled. Smith was killed with an arrow in his back.

An 1832 eulogy in the Illinois Monthly called Jedediah Smith "a man whom none could approach without respect, and whom none could know without esteem."

Chapter 5

The Origin of Gold

'One cubic foot of gold weighs more than one-half ton'

I know two men who understand the true value of gold— unfortunately they disagree.
Baron von Rothschild

While the gold rush brought thousands of anxious prospectors to California in search of the metal, it's doubtful that many gold seekers actually know how gold originates.

The history of gold begins in remote antiquity. Experts in fossil study have observed that bits of natural gold were found in Spanish caves used by the Paleolithic Man about 40,000 B.C.

Historians disagree on the origin of the metal. For instance, while one historian says gold's recorded discovery occurred circa 6000 B.C., another claims the pharaohs and temple priests first used the metal for adornment in ancient Egypt around 3,000 B.C.

U.S. gold reserves in Fort Knox

Gold stored at Fort Knox
(Google Images)

Geologists say the earth was once a mass of hot melted rock. As it cooled, the earth formed different layers. The world's population lives on the outer layer, which is called the crust.

Under this crust is a layer that is still partly melted, called the "outer mantle." This outer mantle contains many minerals, such as gold, silver, and quartz.

As the earth cooled, its crust heaved and cracked. The melted rock seeped up through these cracks and hardened. Naturally, some of this melted rock contained gold, silver, and other minerals.

Some gold is found in certain "veins" of rock, also called "lodes." Some veins are pure gold, but most gold was left mixed together with quartz and other rock. As the planet aged, volcanoes erupted and the earth's crust wrinkled, forming mountain ranges.

Rains, winds, and storms eroded the land. Ancient rivers carved mountain valleys, then changed their course or dried up completely. Parts of the earth's crust collided with other parts, causing powerful earthquakes.

All of these upheavals exposed and broke apart the rock that holds the gold deposits. Rivers that formed and cut through the mountains tore gold from its veins. Chunks of rock washed downstream and broke into gravel.

Erosion wore gravel into sand. Wherever water flowed, it carried bits of gold mixed with gravel and sand.

Gold is very dense, and much heavier than sand or gravel. As gold-bearing rocks were ground apart by water in streams, flakes and nuggets of heavy gold sank into cracks in streambeds. The gold found in streams is called "placer" deposits.

It is curious that ancient Egyptian's medium of exchange was not gold, but barley. The first use of gold as money was probably in 700 B.C. by the citizens of the Kingdom of Lydia (western Turkey).

In 1792, the U.S. Congress adopted a bimetallic standard (gold and silver) for the new nation's currency. Gold was valued at $19.30 per troy ounce. This price remained unchanged until 1834, when the price of gold was raised to the $20.67 level that held for the next 100 years. It was not until 1934 that President Franklin Delano Roosevelt devalued the dollar by raising the price of gold to $35 per ounce.

Gold is the oldest precious metal known to man. Why is it considered so precious? Ancient Egyptians observed that gold's value was a function of its pleasing physical characteristics and its scarcity.

Its physical aspects allow it to be hammered into very thin sheets, or drawn into a fine wire. It is the most malleable of all metals.

It is so malleable that a goldsmith can hammer one ounce of gold into a thin translucent wafer covering more than 100 square feet only five millionths of an inch thick. It would be so thin that 1,000 sheets would be needed to make up the thickness of a single newspaper page.

One ounce of gold can be drawn into a wire 50 miles long. Only one ounce of gold metal is required to plate a thread of copper 1,000 miles long.

Gold is one of the heaviest metals known. It has a specific gravity of 19.3, which means it weighs as much as an equal volume of water. One cubic foot of gold weighs 1,206 pounds.

The heavy weight of gold may explain why there have never been any really large armed robberies of gold bullion. It is too heavy for most robbers to carry in great amounts.

Scientists figure that in all recorded history, only about 120,000 metric tons has been collected. The total hoard of the world's gold will occupy a single cube 60 feet by 60 feet by 60 feet. Gold's scarcity is one thing that makes is so valuable.

According to author Timothy McNulty, more gold was taken from California's American River and its tributaries than all other rivers and streams in the state combined.

The word "placer" is believed to originate from either a Spanish nautical term meaning "sandbank" or a more common usage meaning, "pleasure."

Gold was not first discovered in California in 1848 as history so avidly contends. Sir Francis Drake, who touched on California's coast in 1579, reported that gold was "occurring in abundance." Other finds have been reported in California for the years 1775, 1812, 1814, and 1824.

Chapter 6

Chinese Save Railroads

When American workers left their railroad jobs to pan for gold, it was Chinese workers that brought the Intercontinental Railroad to fruition. (Google Images)

Chinese workman proved vital in building California's early railroads. All other potential workers had left for the gold fields. One of the earliest employers of Chinese was the California Central Railroad, which was extending a line from Sacramento to Marysville.

From the Chinese Historical Society of America's archives comes the following newspaper item, printed in the *Sacramento Union* in 1858:

Two years after the beginning of construction, less than 50 miles of running track had been completed. Construction superintendent J.H. Strobridge needed 5,000 laborers, but the largest force he could muster any time during the spring of 1885 was 800.

When it was suggested to Strobridge that Chinese workers be hired, Strobridge was adamant, "I will not boss Chinese. I will not be responsible for work done on the road by Chinese labor."

As the labor situation grew more critical, Strobridge was forced to relent. He decided to experiment by hiring fifty Chinese workers from the vicinity, restricting them to tasks such as filling dump carts.

The Chinese proved so adept at the task they were soon given the duty of driving the carts as well as loading them. Still not sure the Oriental workers were capable of really hard physical labor, Strobridge tried using them on softer excavations, with excellent results.

Convinced, the superintendent began hiring Chinese workers in earnest. Railroad agents scoured the towns of California for Chinese laborers. By the fall of 1865, there were 3,000 Chinese on the payroll.

Soon, four men in every five hired by the Central Pacific were Chinese. When the supply of local Chinese labor was exhausted, the railroad began recruiting in the Far East. The number of Chinese workers increased to ten or eleven thousand by the time the golden spike was placed May 10, 1869.

According to the Chinese Historical Society of America, Chinese workers were divided into gangs of 12 to 20 each. Each group had a cook. His job was not only to prepare meals, but also to have a large boiler of hot water ready each night so the workers could take a hot sponge bath and change their cloths before their evening meal.

Each gang also had a "head man". Each evening he received from the foreman an account of the time credited to his gang. The head man in turn divided it among the individuals. The head man also bought and paid for all provisions used by his gang. At the end of each month, he collected the amount due him from each individual.

Hours of work were from sunrise to sunset, six days per week. Initially, the wages of the Chinese workers were set at one dollar per day or twenty-six dollars per month. Later, this was raised to thirty dollars, and finally to thirty-five dollars per month. After expenses were deducted, each man had $20 to $30 left.

The Chinese historical society notes the railroad probably relied on Chinese merchants for advice on what to feed the workers.

They were fed a Chinese diet including dried oysters, dried cuttle fish, dried fish, sweet rice, crackers, dried bamboo, salted cabbage, Chinese sugar, dried fruits and vegetables, vermicelli, dried seaweed, Chinese bacon, dried abalone, dried mushrooms, peanut oil, tea, rice, pork, and poultry.

The railroad company provided the workers with low cloth tents, but many preferred to live in dugouts or to burrow into the earth.

These workers soon set an example for diligence, steadiness, and clean living. They had few fights and no "blue" Mondays.

California Governor Leland Stanford, also a director of the Central Pacific, wrote the president of the United States on October 10, 1865, the following: "As a class they are quiet, peaceable, patient, industrious and economical. Ready and apt to learn all the different kinds of work required in railroad building, they soon became as efficient as white laborers..."

At one point in the construction of the railroad, the workers faced a particular hazard. The area was known as Cape Horn, a nearly perpendicular promontory. The American River ran 1,400 feet below.

Chinese workmen were lowered from the top of the cliff in safety harness.. The men, chipped and drilled holes for explosives, then scrambled up the lines while gunpowder exploded beneath. Inch by inch they gouged a roadbed from the granite.

The ordeal of the Chinese workers worsened. One year after construction started, the railroad had only reached Cisco, still on the western slope of the Sierra.

Charles Crocker, one of the owners of the rail line, ordered the workers to start tunneling Donner Summit. The Chinese lived practically out of sight of the sky that entire winter. They dug chimneys and airshafts and lived by lantern light. They tunneled their way from their camps to the portal of the tunnel to work long, underground shifts.

Historical society documents relate that soon, a remarkable labyrinth developed under the snow. The corridors in some cases were wide enough to allow two-horse sleds to move through freely. They ranged up to 200 feet long. Through them, workmen traveled back and forth, digging, blasting, and removing the rubble.

Loss of life was considerable. The *Dutch Flat Enquirer* reported on December 25, 1866, that "a gang of Chinamen (sic) employed by the railroad were covered up by a snow slide and 4 or 5 died before they could be exhumed."

When spring arrived, Crocker ordered a massive assault on the summit tunnel. He wrote:

"We had a shaft down in the center. We were cutting both ways from the bottom of the shaft. We got some Cornish miners from Virginia City and paid them extra wages. We put them on one side of the shaft and the Chinese on the other. We measured the work every Sunday morning. The Chinamen (sic) without fail out-measured the Cornish."

Years later, superintendent Strobridge told a federal investigating commission:

"The snow slides carried away our camps and we lost a good many men in these slides; many of them we did not find until the next season when the snow melted."

In mid-1868, the Central Pacific finally broke through the Sierra barrier. The true cost in human lives will probably never be known since few records were kept.

Workers Strike

In June 1867, some 2,000 Chinese engaged in tunnel work in the high Sierra went on strike. Since the Chinese received no support from other workers, the strike collapsed in one week.

The workers were asking for a raise to forty dollars per month. They also wanted the workday in the open to be limited to 10 hours, and that in the tunnels cut to eight hours.

The Chinese also objected to the right of the overseers to whip or restrain them from leaving the railroad when they desired to seek other employment.

This strike so alarmed the railroad that officials wired east for several Negroes as replacements.

Chapter 7

California's First White School Teacher

'She wrote lessons on the dirt floor'

Inside Mission Santa Clara de Asis, the future looked grim for the 130 Americans. The gates of the crumbling Mission were barricaded to keep out the Spanish soldiers of Don Francisco Sanchez, who appeared on the verge of attacking the newly arrived emigrants.

There was a climate of fear inside the mission, especially among the children. Olive Mann Isbell, the niece of Horace Mann and a former teacher herself, could see the children needed both attention and a haven.

She set the children and any others who would volunteer to clean an old 15-foot square foot adobe stable. A rickety table and a few benches were thrown together from scraps of wood left in the compound.

"Before you get started, you'll have to learn how to use this," she was told as one of the men handed her a long rifle. When classes began, she kept the weapon handy.

Olive Mann Isbell
(Author's File Photo)

Mrs. Mann lacked even pencils and paper. She wrote lessons on the dirt floor with a long pointed stick. From each spent fire she saved the charcoal and wrote the youngsters' A-B-Cs on the palms of their hands. Olive Mann Isbell soon became Aunt Olive to the children, who tried to imitate her courage.

Thus began the first school in California taught by an American.

Many of the emigrants in the compound were sick, including Dr. Chauncy Isbell, a medical graduate of Western Reserve College. The Isbells came west with $2000 in reserve funds and a well-fitted wagon.

As they crossed the Sierra Nevada, John Fremont met them at a pass near Bear River and escorted them to Sutter's Fort and then on to the Mission. Dr. Isbell was drafted to join Fremont and his men. However, upon crossing the Salinas River, he was stricken with typhoid pneumonia, the so-called 'emigrant fever' and returned to the Mission.

Olive's knowledge of drugs and nursing served her well as she tended to her ill husband and others suffering sickness. While her patients slept, Olive made bullets to hold off their attackers.

When Dr. Isbell became well enough to travel, he and his wife moved to Monterey. When they arrived, they learned the Mexican War had ended and California was about to become a member of the United States.

On her very first night in Monterey, Thomas O. Larkin, United States Consul, who had heard of her previous school at the Mission, awakened Olive. Larkin wanted her to set up a similar school in Monterey.

Dr. Isbell began a medical practice, and Olive opened a school with about two dozen students. This number soon grew to about fifty, with each student paying six dollars for a term of three months.

Unlike the conditions in the Mission, Olive opened a classroom with a few books, and with some pencils and paper. The school was located above the jail. Only two of her students knew how to speak English.

A tutor helped Mrs. Isbell, who spoke no Spanish. The Isbells soon moved to French Camp, a community near Tuleberg, where Stockton now sits.

They had barely settled when gold was discovered at Sutter's Mill. Dr. Isbell and others organized the Stockton Mining Company and set out for the gold fields.

Once when it was so muddy the horses could not travel on the road, Dr. Isbell showed up with a young boy helping him carry eighty pounds of gold in sacks on their backs.

While Dr. Isbell was away mining, the twenty-four-year-old Olive was left to care for the horses, chickens, milk cows and 600 head of cattle. Her only help was a nine-year-old boy.

She discovered the Indians liked the type of clothing she wore. She made an outfit every day, which she traded for two ounces of gold. She soon found herself cooking meals for travelers, for which she charged a modest sum. She received $500 in gold when she sent a wagon to Stockton filled with two demijohns of milk, two of cream, some eggs, four-dozen chickens, and a few pounds of butter.

By 1850, the Isbells had become wealthy. The couple had no children. Dr. Isbell wanted to travel and convinced his reluctant wife to sell their French Camp holdings.

Eventually, they returned to California and settled in Santa Paula. Olive died there on March 25, 1899.

Chapter 8

First Long-Distance Line

Wells Fargo Office still marks the spot where the community of French Corral existed. (Google Images)

French Corral was named for a mule corral erected in 1849 by a Frenchman, who was the first settler in the area. When rich placers were later discovered nearby, a town quickly appeared on the site of the Frenchman's corral.

It was one of the first of the historic mining camps to spring up along the ancient San Juan River channel. The gravel of the San Juan River channel follows along the ridge for many miles.

These accumulations, washed down over millions of years, contain fossil wood and nearly every kind of rock known to the Sierra region. It also contained gold, and lots of it. Some past geologic events left the deposits high and dry above the present river systems, causing wild speculations among miners as to how the gold got there.

French Corral is now a village of only a few people, but retains its historic flavor.

These accumulations, washed down over millions of years, contain fossil wood and nearly
every kind of rock known to the Sierra region. It also contained gold, and lots of it. Some past geologic events left the deposits high and dry above the present river systems, causing wild speculations among miners as to how the gold got there.

French Corral is now a village of only a few people, but retains its historic flavor.

The long-distance telephone line terminated at the Milton Mining & Water Co. The building has since been torn down.

For several years, the town simply existed, as gold deposits did not appear to be rich.

When hydraulic mining was introduced, everything changed at French Corral. The town boomed as hundreds of miners rushed to the area. French Corral became one of the premier towns of the district, second only to North San Juan in size and importance.

But French Corral is most famous for being the terminus of California's first long distance telephone service. The Milton Mining Company wanted some way to talk to the controllers sixty miles away.

The Ridge Telephone Line was strung from French Corral, near Nevada City, to Milton, in neighboring Sierra County. In Milton, the line was connected to the Western Union Telegraph Company line, which was connected to the rest of the United States.

The Ridge Line was hung on trees and poles that connected twenty-two stations.

The phone line was a private line but if someone wanted to use it, a toll of fifty cents for twenty words was collected.

There was a booster station built at Malakoff Mine. A homemade battery was made from six quart jars held together and filled with mixtures of manganese, sal ammonia, blue stone, and zinc. The booster allowed the phone line to continue to the full sixty miles.

After 1884, when hydraulic mining was ordered stopped, federal inspectors would arrive from Marysville to check the mines. The phone line was used to signal the arrival of strangers.

Miners were alerted to stop the hydraulic mining before the inspectors would arrive. In Downieville, the miners were notified of strangers in town by hanging a pair of stuffed overalls on the Saint Charles Hotel flag pole.

Today, the telephone line, which operated for 20 years, is a California historical landmark.

The Milton Mining & Water Co., in which one terminus of the long-distance telephone line was connected, has long been torn down.

Chapter 9

The Water Race

'Two factions wanted to develop the river'

Julius Howells was an engineer who looked at the 50 square miles of the rolling expanse of high meadow with a gleam in his eye.

His particular interest was a point where the Feather River flowed out of the valley through a narrow gorge and began its steep descent into the Feather River Canyon.

A dam across that gorge, Howells envisioned, would convert Big Meadows into a superb storage reservoir. Howells vision in the early 1880s planted the seed that would later grow into Great Western Power Company.

There were indeed obstacles to scale before his dream could be realized. First was the matter of funding such a project. It wasn't until 1901 that Howells received the backing of Edwin T. Earl, of Los Angeles, and his brother, Guy C. Earl, of Oakland, to develop what would be the finest hydroelectric site in all of California.

The water flowing from the Feather River became the monumental prize in a water race
(Google Images)

With funding in place, Howells and Augustus R. Bidwell began posting water-appropriation notices along the Feather River.

Lake Almanor is the result of the damming of the Feather River. (Google Images)

While posting the notices, they surprisingly encountered H.F. Lange, promoter, and N.B. Kellogg, a civil engineer, posting similar notices.

Thus the race began. Bidwell leaped into a spring wagon and hurtled along the barely discernible mountain road, closely followed, moments later, by another sleigh with Lange and Kellogg in hot pursuit.

This was indeed an important race, for the winner would claim rights to the water of the Feather River for power production.

The 31-mile bone-jarring race ended with Bidwell arriving at Quincy 40 minutes ahead of Lange and Kellogg. Howells had stayed behind to post more notices. Bidwell filed his papers with the county recorder at 8:25 p.m., and he and Howells shared in the great prize of which was later to become Lake Almanor.

With Big Meadows land and water now assured, the Earl Brothers incorporated Western Power Company in 1902. They then began the task of finding powerhouse sites.

Their first site was one at Big Bend, 65 miles downriver from Big Meadows and about 16 miles from Oroville. Here the river made a great sweeping loop, its downstream end only three miles from the upstream end, and with a tunnel already driven through this narrow neck.

The tunnel, it is said, was the work of patent medicine king Ray V. Pierce, whose "Dr. Pierce" signs once covered barn roofs across the nation. Pierce's gold mining scheme involving the tunnel had not worked out and he was ready to sell.

Work began immediately at Big Bend. Dr. Pierce's tunnel was reamed out to a larger diameter and extended to provide a fall of water of 465 feet. The first 10,000-kilowatt unit went into operation in December 1908. Later, five more units were added to bring total capacity to 70,000 kilowatts.

This powerhouse depended on the natural flow of the river until a dam at Big Meadows could be built. Workmen began building a multiple-arch dam in 1910. After five of the planned 22 concrete arches were finished, the builders found they had to go much deeper through a seam of clay to find bedrock than had been expected.

Word of this obstacle leaked out, and a first-class controversy arose. Guy Earl then announced the concrete dam would be abandoned.

A hydraulic-filled dam was begun upstream under the supervision of engineer Julius Howells, one of the originators of this type construction. Sand, gravel and clay were poured between the canyon wall to form a core, with more sand and gravel on the outside slopes.

The first dam was finished in 1914. It was 72 feet high from streambed to crest and extended 650 feet from one canyon wall to the other. A reservoir of 220,000 acre-feet was created.

Howells named the lake for the three daughters of Great Western Power Company's Guy C. Earl. He used syllables of each of the daughters' names, which were ALice, MArtha, and EliNORe. Howells mistakenly thought the last daughter spelled her name "Eleanor" when he devised the name of the lake. Lake Almanor, nevertheless, kept its name.

Chapter 10

Marshall Tells How He Found Gold

(This first-hand account is said to be James Marshall's first version of his finding gold at Coloma. It appeared in "Gold Rush, A Literary Exploration," published by California Council for the Humanities. His language has not been edited.)

"In May, 1847, with my rifle, blanket, and a few crackers to eat with the venison (for the deer were awful plenty), I ascended the American River, according to Mr. (John) Sutter's wish, as he wanted to find a good site for a saw mill, where we could have plenty of timber, and where wagons would be able to ascend and descend the river hills.

"Many fellows had been out before me, but they could not find any place to suit, so when I left I told Mr. Sutter I would go along the river to its very head and find the place, if such a place existed anywhere upon the river or any of its forks. traveled along the river the whole way. Many places would suit very well for the erection of the mill, with plenty of timber everywhere, but then nothing but a mule could climb the hills; and when

In his words, James Marshall tells his reaction when he found gold in the tail race of the lumber mill he was building. (Google Images)

I would find a spot where the hills were not steep, there was no timber to be had; and so it was until I had been out several days and reached this place

(Coloma), which after first sight, looked like the exact spot we were hunting.

"You may be sure Mr. Sutter was pleased when I reported my success. We entered into a partnership; I was to build the mill, and he was to find provisions, teams, tools, and to pay a portion of the men's wages. I believe I was at that time the only millwright in the whole country. In August, everything being ready, we freighted two wagons with tools and provisions, and accompanied by six men I left the fort, and after a good deal of difficulty reached the place one beautiful afternoon and formed our camp on yon rise of ground right above the town.

"Our first business was to put up log houses, as we intended remaining here all winter. This was done in less than no time, for my men were great with the ax. We then cut timber and fell to work hewing it for the framework of the mill. The Indians gathered about us in great numbers. I employed about forty of them to assist us with the dam, which we put up in a kind of way in about four weeks...I left for the fort (after) giving orders to Mr. Weimar to have a ditch cut through the bar in the rear of the mill, and after quitting work in the evening to raise the gate and let the water run all night, as it would assist us very much in deepening and widening the tail-race.

"I returned in a few days, and found everything favorable, all the men being at work in the ditch. When the channel opened it was my custom every evening to raise the gate and let the water wash out as much sand and gravel through the night as possible; and in the morning, while the men were getting breakfast, I would walk down, and, shutting off the water, look along the race and see what was to be done, so that I might tell Mr. Weimar, who had charge of the Indians, at what particular point to set them to work for the day. As I was the only millwright present, all of my time was employed upon the framework and machinery.

"One morning in January—it was a clear, cold morning, I shall never forget that morning—as I was taking my usual walk along the race after shutting off the water, my eye was caught with the glimpse of something shining in the bottom of the ditch. There was about a foot of water running then. I reached my hand down and picked it up; it made my heart thump, for I was certain it was gold. The piece was about half the size and of the shape of a pea. Then I saw another piece in the water. After taking it out I sat down and began to think right hard. I thought it was gold, and yet it did not seem to be of the right color; all the gold coin I had seen was of a reddish tinge; this looked more like brass. I recalled to mind all the metals I had ever seen or heard of, but I could find none that resembled this.

"Suddenly the idea flashed across my mind that it might be iron pyrites. I trembled to think of it! This question could soon be determined. Putting one of the pieces on a hard river stone, I took another and commenced hammering it. It was soft, and didn't break: it therefore must be gold, but largely mixed with some other metal, very likely silver, for pure gold, I thought, would certainly have a brighter color.

"When I returned to our cabin for breakfast I showed the two pieces to my men. They were all a good deal excited, and had they not thought that the gold only existed in small quantities they would abandon everything and left me to finish my job alone. However, to satisfy them, I told them that as soon as we had the mill finished we would devote a week or two to gold hunting and see what we could make out of it.

"While we were working in the race after this discovery we always kept a sharp lookout, and in the course of three or four days we had picked up three ounces—our work still progressing as lively as ever, for none of us imagined at that time that the whole country was sowed with gold.

"In about a week's time after the discovery I had to take another trip to the fort; and, to gain what information I could respecting the real value of the metal, took all we had collected with me and showed it to Mr. Sutter, who at once declared it was gold, but thought with me that it was greatly mixed with some other metal. It puzzled us a good deal to hit upon the means of telling the exact quantity of gold contained in the alloy; however, we at last stumbled on an old American encyclopedia, where we saw the specific gravity of all the metals, and rules given to find the quantity of each in a given bulk.*/

"After hunting over the whole fort and borrowing from some of the men, we got three dollars and a half in silver, and with a small pair of scales we soon ciphered it out that there was no silver nor copper in the gold, but that it was entirely pure.

"This fact being ascertained, we thought it our best policy to keep it as quiet as possible till we should have finished our mill. But there were a great number of disbanded Mormon soldiers in and about the fort, and when they came to hear of it, why it just spread like wildfire, and soon the whole country was in a bustle. I had scarcely arrived at the mill again till several persons appeared with pans, shovels, and hoes, and those that had not iron picks had wooden ones, all anxious to fall to work and dig up our mill; but this we would not permit. As fast as one party disappeared another would arrive, and sometimes I had the greatest kind of trouble to get rid of them. I sent them all off in different directions, telling them about such and such places, where I was certain there was plenty of gold if they would only take the trouble of looking for it. At that time I never imagined that the gold was so abundant. I told them to go to such and such places, because it appeared that they would not dig nowhere but in such places as I pointed out, and I believe such was their confidence in me that they would have dug on the very top of yon mountain if I had told them to do so.

"The second place where gold was discovered was in a gulch near the Mountaineer House, on the road to Sacramento. The third place was on a bar on the South Fork of the American River a little above the junction of the Middle and South forks. The diggings at Hangtown (now Placerville) were discovered next by myself, for we all went out for a while as soon as our job was finished. The Indians next discovered the diggings at Kelsey's and thus in a very short time we discovered that the whole country was but one bed of gold. So there, stranger, is the entire history of the gold discovery in California—a discovery that hasn't as yet been of much benefit to me."

Chapter 11

The Sydney Ducks

Vigilantes hunt out the Sydney Ducks in San Francisco. (Google Images)

San Francisco's Barbary Coast became the destination for a great number of former members of Great Britain's prison colony in Australia. By June of 1849, eight ships had left Sydney, bringing this rough crowd to California, where they soon became known as the "Sydney Ducks."

After one of the forays by the gang, San Francisco residents would comment, "The Sydney Ducks are cackling."

These undesirable aliens washing into the state were, for all intents and purposes, one hundred percent criminal. Their entry into California, which was still under Mexican rule, violated Mexican law, which forbade entry into the territory of any persons who had been convicted of crime in other countries.

Little or no effort had ever been made to enforce the old Mexican statute. Consequently, by early autumn of 1849 the arrivals from Australia became so numerous, and so thoroughly dominated the underworld that the district in which they congregated became known as Sydney Town, a name it held for ten years.

The Australians were often called the Sydney Coves, but were more popularly known as the Sydney Ducks.

The area where the Sydney Ducks congregated later became known as the Barbary Coast. Most of them gathered along the waterfront at Broadway and Pacific Street and on the slopes of Telegraph Hill.

Some of the Sydney Ducks opened lodging houses, dance halls, groggeries, and taverns. Many establishments in San Francisco bore such names as Magpie, the Bobby Burns, the Tam O'Shanter, the Noggin of Ale, the Hilo Johnny, the

Bird-in-Hand, the Bay of Biscay, and the Jolly Waterman.

The city purchased the abandoned brig Euphemia to house the excess Sydney Duck prisoners.
(Google Images)

One journalist viewing the area wrote that all of the so-called taverns were "hives of dronish criminals, shabby little dens with rough, hangdog fellows hanging about doorways."

"Drunkenness, robbery, and all manner of strife and lewdness went on in these places," author Herbert Asbery wrote in his 1933 book, "The Barbary Coast,". "Most of them had harlots regularly attached to the establishment, and these women either sold their favors for a pinch or two of gold dust, or engaged in immoral and peculiar exhibitions, admission to which ranged from fifty cents to five dollars."

Any upstanding individual venturing into the den of thieves area rarely escaped without being beaten and robbed.

According to the San Francisco Herald, "There are certain spots in our city, infested by the most abandoned men and women, that have acquired a reputation little better than the Five Points of New York or St. Giles of London."

The paper continued, "The upper part of Pacific Street, after dark, is crowded by thieves, gamblers, low women, drunken sailors, and similar characters, who resort to the groggeries that line the street, and there spend the night in the most hideous orgies."

Unsuspecting sailors and miners are entrapped by the conniving thieves and swindlers where they are filled with liquor—or drugged if necessary—allowing them to become easy prey.

One of the most notorious dives in Sydney Town was the Boar's Head, where the principal attraction was a sexual exhibition in which a woman and a boar participated.

Author Asbery wrote, "The Goat and Compass was the particular hangout of a character known as Dirty Tom McAlear. For a few cents, he would eat or drink any sort of refuse offered to him."

McAlear was finally arrested in 1852 for "making a beast of himself." He testified that he had been drunk for at least seven years and had not bathed for so long that he had no memory of it, although he estimated it might have been 15 years before in England.

In one bar, known for its milk punches, it is said that a San Francisco preacher was conducting a survey of the district to obtain material for a sermon. He was given a milk punch, amply laced with gin.

"What do you call that? He asked the bartender.

"Just milk," was the reply.

"Ah!" said the preacher. "What a glorious cow!"

It wasn't until John W. Geary was chosen as First Alcalde of San Francisco that any attempt was made at bringing order to the city. Geary immediately appeared before the *Ayuntamiento*, or Town Council, and urged the body to take immediate steps for the protection of life and property.

Politicians in San Francisco were better known for their political payoffs and dishonesty than for their actions to make the city a better town. One wag mused, "The best that could be said about any one of them is he probably would not steal a red-hot stove."

Fearful that people would take matters into their own hands, the Ayuntamiento appropriated sufficient money to purchase the brig *Euphemia,* which had been abandoned in the Bay when its crew deserted to go to the mines.

For several years, the vessel was used as a prison. It was San Francisco's first but not very efficient jail. It was described as being "about as useful for the purpose as a chicken-coop would have been."

Soon, an ordinance was enacted requiring the dives and dance halls of Sydney Town to close at midnight. These, however, proved to be futile gestures, which neither Geary or the town council was able to enforce.

"During the half-dozen years that followed Alcalde Geary's first attempt to form a reputable municipal government, an average of almost two murders a day were committed in San Francisco—and at no time during that period did the city have a population of more than forty thousand.

Of more concern to San Francisco residents was the series of fires that had nearly demolished the city. Six times in less than two years, arson-set fires created havoc in the city. Investigations clearly indicated that gangs of firebugs had deliberately set four of these fires. Bands of looters followed the fires.

Two former convicts from Australia, Jack Edwards and Ben Lewis, were arrested, but when brought to trial, were freed by venal judges under the sway of crooked politicians, in turn paid off by the villains living in the Barbary Coast.

The condition of affairs in San Francisco brought about the formation of the first Vigilance

Committee. It was formed June 10, 1850, and comprised some 200 men.

Their stated policy: "No thief, burglar, incendiary, or assassin shall escape punishment, either by the quibbles of the law, the insecurity of the prisons, the carelessness or corruption of the police, or a laxity of those who pretend to administer justice."

Hours after its formation, the committee was called upon to contend with one John Jenkins, a former convict from Australia. Jenkins had burglarized a shipping office on Commercial Street, defying anyone to stop him as he carried away the strongbox.

When Vigilante members tried to stop him, he threw the strongbox into San Francisco Bay in an act of further contempt.

In a hasty trial, Jenkins was promptly found guilty. He was taken to Portsmouth Square by Vigilantes and hanged on the spot.

The Vigilantes continued imposing their brand of justice on gang terrorists despite the actions of San Francisco's appointed sheriff. In one case, two men, Samuel Whittaker and Robert McKenzie were brought to trial, where they confessed their crimes. The Vigilantes sentenced them to die.

The sheriff stepped in, seized the prisoners, and put them in jail. The disgruntled Vigilantes would not hear of it. They abducted the pair again and took them to their headquarters. As the firehouse bell announced the execution of

Whittaker and McKenzie, six thousand people watched.

Vigilante activity lasted only two years. The final entry in the Vigilante secretary's record book was dated June 30, 1852. However, similar vigilante activity soon extended to the mining camps, and the self-appointed lawmen were especially heavy-handed in imposing sentences against foreigners.

In Downieville, a mining town on the Yuba River, a group of American Independence Day celebrants decided to impose their authority on Juanita, considered an "evil" Mexican woman.

Juanita fought back, killing one of the Vigilante members with a knife. She was hastily found guilty and hung from a wooden bridge spanning the Yuba River. There were some miners on the jury who were repelled by the idea of hanging a woman.

Punishment by Vigilante sometimes involved branding, ear cropping, and whipping.

Chapter 12

The Wreck of the Winfield Scott

'It smacked into Anacapa Island'

California's hide and tallow trade was augmented by a steady stream of steamers plying the Panama Route. This route was the most popular way to reach California's gold fields before the completion of the first transcontinental railroad in 1869.

The Pacific Mail Steamship Company started operating in 1848. As the number of both its ships and its competitors grew, the emphasis for ship's captains was intense.

The Winfield Scott was one such vessel and was a part of the newly formed New York and San Francisco Steamship Line. The Winfield Scott set a record when it made the trip from New York to San Francisco, traveling via Rio de Janeiro and Cape Horn in less than 49 days.

The ship was named for the commanding general of the United State Army, who was also a hero of the Mexican War.

The steamship Winfield Scott crashed into Anacapa Island. (Google Images)

Certainly the passengers and crew did not anticipate this trip would be its final voyage. It had departed San Francisco with a full load of passengers and a shipment of gold bullion. The date was December 1, 1853.

Because "time was money" to the steamship lines, the ship's captain, Simon F. Blunt, elected to travel through the Santa Barbara Channel rather than a passage outside the islands. He had not anticipated the bank of heavy fog that shrouded the area as he entered the channel.

According to author James Delgado, who did extensive research about the ship's voyage, the captain evidently intended to steam between Anacapa and Santa Cruz islands. Instead, he piled into Middle Anacapa Island at full speed, estimated at about 10 knots. The time was eleven o'clock in the evening.

Confusion was high on board the Winfield Scott side-wheeler. Asa C. Call was a passenger on the Winfield Scott. In his dairies, he writes:

"I had just got to sleep, when I was awakened by a tremendous shock. I knew we had struck a rock and hurrying on a part of my clothes, I hurried up on deck where I found a general panic. The steamer was backed off and with the assurance that all was right the most of the passengers retired again to their rooms.

"But I didn't believe she could have struck a rock with such force without sustaining some injury, and not knowing what the upshot of the matter might be, I went down to my stateroom and put my money and all other valuables in my trunk into my saddle bags, and went into the upper saloon (sic) intending to be ready for what was to come next.

"I had hardly taken a seat when the steamer struck again, and with such force that it seemed as if the ship was breaking into a thousand fragments. I again hurried on deck and went forward to see if I could see land. It was so dark I could see nothing, but I could distinctly hear the roar of breakers ahead, and on the larboard side. The steamer was unmanageable, and the order was given to let off the steam and to extinguish the fires to prevent the ship's taking fire."

Call said that about ten minutes after the second crash, a longboat was launched, which was evidence the Winfield Scott was sinking.

"I heard the captain call for the ladies to go aboard. Some men pressed towards the boat but the Captain's orders were 'knock the first man overboard that attempts to get into the boat.'"

Call's dairies noted there was a great breach in the steamer and water was pouring in like a river. "Our only hope was that she might not sink entirely, as we could feel her sliding down the side of a ledge of rocks.

"Pretty soon," his dairy continued, "the fog began to break away a little and we could see the light in the long boat as she was along in search of a landing. We could also see the top of a high peak just ahead of the ship and pretty near, but it seemed perpendicular and the white foam and the roar showed that we could never hope to land there.

Call said, "As soon as the life preservers were distributed, the other ships boats (five) were lowered, and filled with passengers. They all held about one hundred and fifty, and there were five hundred and twenty on board. After being gone about half an hour the long boat returned, having found a landing. And in about two hours, all hands were taken off, and were landed on a rock about fifty yards long by twenty five wide."

The passengers were transferred to the island proper the next morning. The group was forced to camp there for the entire following week. Finally, the ship *California* arrived to carry the passengers on to Panama.

The ship's company, author Delgado wrote, remained on the island for two more days, concentrating on the recovery of the mail and baggage that was carried on board. Besides mail and luggage, there were some furniture, machinery and foodstuffs aboard.

Captain Horatio Gates Trussell, of Santa Barbara, salvaged wood that became incorporated into the home now preserved as the Trussell-Winchester Adobe. The home also includes two brass thresholds from the ship.

Major salvage of the ship occurred in 1894 when the ship *San Pedro* came to the site and removed several hundred copper bolts and much of the iron machinery.

Sport divers in recent years have been attracted to the wreck by the recovery of gold coins. Park officials, however, have focused some of their efforts on prosecuting violations of antiquity laws, which now protect the wreck's contents.

The only piece of the wreckage, which stands above the bottom of the sea, is the shaft of what is interpreted as the port paddlewheel.

The Winfield Scott was first launched in October, 1850, and began operations on the route between New Orleans and New York. At the beginning of 1852, it became a part of the New York and San Francisco Steamship Line.

Chapter 13

The Pelton Wheel

'His water turbine wrung energy from each drop of water'

The Pelton Wheel

When mine owners needed a more efficient water wheel to run their stamp mills, they decided to have a contest.

They called for a test of all water wheels made along the Pacific Coast. Representatives of four major companies readied their wheels for the competition along a stream in Grass Valley.

None seemed to care about Lester Pelton, who was also setting up his wheel in that summer of 1883.

Pelton was unschooled and less sophisticated than the officials the of other four water wheel companies competing in the power contest. He had patented his unconventional water wheel three years earlier, but so far, had been unable to convince any water user to try it.

University of California's engineering department at Berkeley had recently tested Pelton's wheel. Their results showed that Pelton might hold a few surprises when the energy tests for the mining companies were run.

When the Grass Valley test day arrived, it appeared to observers that each wheel looked to be moving very fast, and the suspense built as mine officials huddled to compare the results.

A spokesman announced the results. "Pelton's wheel wins hands down. Its rating is 87.3 percent. That's 19 percentage points ahead of the runner-up."

Everyone was surprised except Pelton.

Born in 1829 in Vermillion, Ohio, Pelton came to California in 1850 with the gold rush migrants and became a fisherman on the Sacramento River. After three years, he gave up on fishing and began working in the gold mines of Camptonville, Nevada City and Grass Valley. He later became a carpenter and a millwright.

The slow and inefficient water wheels used in the flourmills were not fast enough for the gold miners. They installed turbines, or wheels with cups around their circumference, on which a jet of water was directed, forcing it to turn.

For centuries, water wheels, rimmed by flat paddles, were turned by water flowing in rivers and millstreams. The best of these "hurdy gurdies" achieved was about 40 percent efficiency.

Eventually, buckets replaced the flat paddles on the water wheel, and the water was channeled through pipes and a nozzle. The wheel's efficiency rose to about 65 percent. Still, the water slowed the wheel as it splashed backwards from each bucket, cutting down on efficiency.

Pelton began experimenting in a shed behind his landlady's house in Camptonville. Working with small experimental wheels, he tested them at night when the demand for water ebbed. Over time, he devised more than 40 models, including one that powered the landlady's washing machine.

Sometime in the 1870s, Lester Pelton was watching a spinning water turbine when the key holding its wheel onto its shaft slipped, causing it to become misaligned.

Instead of the jet of water hitting the cups in their middle, the slippage caused it to hit near the edge of the cups. Rather than the water flow being stopped, it was now deflected into a half-circle, coming out of the cup again in a reversed direction.

"Hmmm," Pelton thought. "That's funny."

As he watched, he said, "That's the answer."

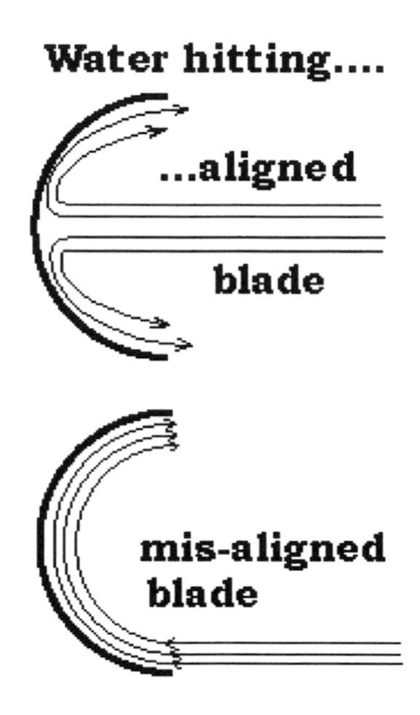

He rushed to his shop to experiment. The result in 1878 was a prototype of a simple, durable, amazingly efficient wheel. Pelton obtained his patent for the idea in 1880.

The beauty of Pelton's invention, according to an article in a copy of a PG&E Progress newsletter, is its ability to make full use of a small amount of water falling a long way.

Pelton's wheel proved a big success in the rugged Sierra, first for the gold mining companies and then, with the coming of long-distance transmission lines, for the electric utility industry.

Orders for his wheel outstripped the capacity of foundries near Camptonville, so Pelton headed for San Francisco. With local backing, he formed the Pelton Water Wheel Company in 1888. By 1895, there were 850 companies using his improved wheels.

Chapter 14

Father of California Wine Industry

Agoston Haraszthy is considered the father of California's wine industry. He developed the first high-quality grape vineyard at Crystal Springs in San Mateo County. (Google Images)

Agoston Haraszthy made an impression wherever he went. After serving as a member of the Royal Hungarian Guards of Francis I, Emperor of Austria-Hungary in 1830, he was forced to flee Europe for fear of being branded a revolutionist.

In 1842, he returned to Hungary and convinced his father to liquidate their considerable holdings so the entire family could immigrate to America. When they arrived in Sauk City, Wisconsin, they were among the best-capitalized immigrants of the 19th century.

Along with his other entrepreneurial investments, Haraszthy began agricultural experiments and achieved considerable success in sheep raising and growing hops.

Even with his considerable success, he was still disappointed at not being able to establish the high quality vineyards of his native Hungary. The tug of the western frontier pulled at the Haraszthy family, and they headed, by wagon train, to California in 1848.

Agoston was the wagon master of the train, which included about sixty immigrants. Without serious incident, the wagon train arrived at Warner Hot Springs, in San Diego County.

Colonel Jonathan Warner, a former militiaman who established Warner Hot Springs in 1844, apprised Haraszthy about the agriculture and the politics in the San Diego area. A scant 650 people, mainly vaqueros, Yankee sailors who had jumped ship, and a few Mormon soldiers from the Mormon Battalion populated San Diego.

Haraszthy's family now included his wife, six children, his father and stepmother, and Thomas

W. Sutherland, former U.S. Attorney for Wisconsin Territory, who was now Haraszthy's stepbrother.

The Polish immigrant purchased a plot of land adjacent to San Luis Rey Mission, and, with his sons, Attila and Arpad, first planted a large fruit orchard. He later bought 160 acres more in Mission Valley and planted peach and cherry trees sent to him from New York State.

Haraszthy never ceased his investment activity as well as his interest in community politics. With Don Juan Bandini, Haraszthy set up the first regularly scheduled omnibus transit system and established a livery stable. He established a very profitable butcher shop.

With other real estate speculators, he helped establish the subdivision of Middletown. Haraszthy Street existed there until the early 1960s when it was wiped from the map by the construction of Interstate 5.

When San Diego County was chartered in 1850, Haraszthy was elected the first City Marshall, while his father, Charles, was elected Magistrate and Land Commissioner. His stepbrother, Tom Sutherland, became San Diego's first City Attorney.

In 1851, he was elected to the State Assembly and resigned his other offices. While in the legislature, then meeting in Vallejo, Haraszthy succeeded in getting funding for the expansion of San Diego Harbor and the county's first public hospital.

He was the first legislator to introduce legislation to divide California into two states; North and South. Because of powerful political interest in Northern California, that bill died.

All the while, Haraszthy continued searching for land more suitable for agriculture than San Diego's subtropical desert land offered. Early in 1852, he purchased 210 acres near San Francisco's Mission Dolores. He moved the entire family there at the end of the Assembly Session.

Haraszthy's noteworthy accomplishments didn't stop. He introduced the "Zinfandel" red wine grape and the "Muscat of Alexandria" raisin grape to California.

He invented an efficient gold refining process, and was founding partner in the Eureka Gold and Silver Refining Company. The firm became one of the major contract refiners for the San Francisco Mint.

Because of his reputation for fairness and honesty, Haraszthy was appointed Assayer of the Mint in 1855.

He developed the first large, high-quality grape vineyard at Crystal Springs in San Mateo County. At this new ranch, Haraszthy designed and laid out a nursery and horticultural garden, which he named Los Flores.

With his son's help, he planted fruit trees and shrubs imported from the east. At about this same time, he received a shipment of six choice rooted vines and 160 cuttings from Hungary.

In the shipment were two small bundles. One was the Muscat of Alexandria and the other was said to be the famous mystery grape, the Zinfandel. Today the Zinfandel is the most widely planted wine grape in California.

In 1857, while visiting General Mariano Guadalupe Vallejo at the General's Lachrima Montis estate, Haraszthy was introduced to the Sonoma Valley. This valley especially appealed to him because its weather, topography and soil were so similar to his Hungarian homeland's high quality vineyards.

In Sonoma, he established the Szeptaj Estate (Buena Vista). That Buena Vista Winery is today a state park and historical site.

In 1861, He was appointed to a California commission to improve agricultural methods and to collect vines and fruit tree stocks in Europe. During a European tour with his son, Arpad, he purchased, with his own money, 100,000 grapevines representing 1,400 varieties, along with small selected lots of planting stock for olives, almonds, pomegranates, oranges, lemons and chestnuts.

When he returned, Harper & Brothers, of New York, published Haraszthy's report, "Grape Culture, Wines and Wine Making upon Agriculture and Horticulture. It remained the winemaking classic authority in the English language until well into the 20th century.

The Haraszthy family planted vineyards for European immigrant friends and wine growers, including Charles Krug, Emile Dreser and Jacob Grundlach.

In 1863, Agoston's sons Attila and Arpad Haraszthy were married in a double ceremony to the twin daughters of General Vallejo.

Chapter 15

Butterfield Overland Mail

The mail went through in 25 days.
(Google Images)

When California was admitted as a state in 1850, mail left the East Coast by boat and sailed all the way around the southern tip of South America and back up to California. Delivery took weeks.

In early 1857, the Post Office Department called for bids on a contract for an overland mail route to California. Stipulated in the contract was that delivery time could not exceed 25 days, and the route must run twice a week.

John Butterfield, who had been a stagecoach driver for some eastern stage lines, was awarded the $600,000 contract, with the starting date to be September 1858. Butterfield spent a year of frantic and grueling effort to get the route planned, built, and equipped.

Butterfield had long experience in the stage line business. He had first been a stage driver, but had risen to ownership of several lines in New York, and in 1850, he had been one of the founders of American Express Company.

He chose St. Louis, Missouri, as his eastern terminal, but by the time he got everything ready to go, the rail line had already reached Tipton, Missouri. By using the railroad line he was able to draw more passengers and reduce his operating costs.

As soon as the contract was signed, Butterfield set out to survey the route he had worked so hard to plan. He sent out agents to hunt out and employ guides, scouts, and frontiersmen who were friendly with the various Indian tribes. These men also had to be well acquainted with every spring, water hole, stream ford and mountain pass along the route.

Butterfield divided his 2,975-mile route into 200 way stations and relay posts. The relay posts were close enough together that the distance could be traveled at a rapid pace under any kind of weather.

The Line faced tremendous obstacles in getting going. A plentiful supply of hay, grain, food, firewood and sleeping and feeding accommodations for passengers had to be built. Bridges had to be built across streams, or ferryboats provided for the larger streams.

Collecting the supplies was a monumental task. Traders went out to buy the toughest, fastest horses and mules available. Concord stagecoaches were ordered, along with heavy freight wagons for hauling thousands of tons of hay and grain.

Butterfield spent more than a million dollars to get the mail route ready for operation.

The mails went through almost without exception in the twenty-five days allowed.

Butterfield told his drivers, "Remember boys, nothing on God's earth must stop the mail."

The postage rate of ten cents per half ounce resulted in receipts in 1860 of $119,766.77. The fare for passengers averaged $200 one-way. He at first planned to carry four passengers. Soon, he was carrying nine passengers, whose knees were locked tightly together inside the coach, with a few more passengers perched on the roof.

The Butterfield Stage Line, with its high cost of moving the mail, could not carry freight at a reasonable cost. When it first began operating, it carried only letters. Later, it added newspapers and small packages.

In 1859, the idea of the Pony Express was conceived, and put into action between St. Louis and Sacramento. It promised unprecedented speed in mail delivery over the almost 2,000 mile route.

The first attempt to carry the mail overland was made by George Chorpenning, who set out in the spring of 1851 with a string of pack mules to haul the mail from Sacramento to Salt Lake City.

The Sierra Nevada crossing proved too much, especially in winter.

The Federal government, in 1857, then authorized the so-called "Jackass Mail," the San Antonio & San Diego Mail Line from Texas to California. The "Jackass Mail" was short-lived, and in March of the same year, Congress authorized the creation of the Butterfield Overland Mail.

Butterfield's Inventory

- 250 Concord Coaches
- 500 other vehicles
- 1800 horses and mules
- 3000 tons of hay and grain
- Food provisions warehoused
- Water available at relay posts
- 1200 skilled superintendents, road bosses, drivers, guards, conductors, harness makers, blacksmiths, keepers, hostlers and clerks.

Chapter 16

Sarah Winchester's Mystery House

Sara Winchester

Some say Sarah Winchester thought that as long as she built onto her house she would not die. Others believed she was only an eccentric rich woman with more money than good sense, along with a poor sense of building design.

There is no doubt about her wealth. When her husband, William Wirt Winchester died, she inherited $20 million in cash inheritance, along with $1,000 per day income.

On the advice of a friend, Sarah had consulted a medium. The fortuneteller told Sarah that her family was cursed by the spirits of all those who had been killed by Winchester rifles, which, by the way, were the source of her wealth.

She built, and built, and built, thinking this would prevent her from dying. (Google Images)

She was further advised to sell her New Haven, Connecticut home and move west. This she did in 1884. She traveled to San Jose, where she found a six-room home under construction. She convinced the owner to sell her the uncompleted home, along with the 162 acres on which it sat.

The house soon grew to include 26 rooms. Eventually, railroad cars were switched onto a nearby siding to bring building materials and imported furnishings to the house.

Sarah met each morning with her foreman to go over her hand-sketched plans for the day's work. According to one writer, "The plans were often chaotic but showed a real flair for building. Sometimes though, they would not work out the right way, but Sarah always had a quick solution. They would just build another room around an existing one."

Eventually, Sarah's house grew to a height of seven stories. Inside the house, three elevators were installed along with 47 fireplaces. Countless staircases led to nowhere, simply going up and ending at a ceiling.

The number 13 intrigued Sarah Winchester. Nearly all of the windows contained 13 panes of glass; the walls had 13 panels; the greenhouse had 13 cupolas; many of the wooden floors contained 13 sections; some of the rooms had 13 windows; and every staircase but one had 13 steps.

It is said that Sarah slept in a different room in the house each night.

The exception is a winding staircase with 42 steps, which would normally be enough to take a climber up three stories. In this case, the steps only rise nine feet because each step is only two inches high.

Her house, it is said, had been designed into a maze to confuse and discourage the bad spirits. Her building allowed her to control the spirits who came to the house to avenge all those men killed by Winchester rifles, the source of her wealth.

Sarah had married William Wirt Winchester. In 1857, he took over the assets of a firm that made the “Volcanic Repeater,” a rifle that used a lever mechanism to load bullets into the breech.

The company soon developed the “Henry Rifle,” which had a tubular magazine under the barrel. It became the true repeating rifle and a favorite among the Northern troops during the Civil War.

Sarah kept 22 carpenters at work, year around, 24-hours a day. For the next 38 years, the building continued, and the house grew in all directions, inside and out.

Even though the house was large and spacious, Sarah never entertained guests. Only she and her servants lived in the house.

The house was badly damaged when the great San Francisco earthquake struck in 1906. Portions of the Winchester house were left in near ruin. The top three stories had collapsed into the gardens and would never be rebuilt.

On September 4, 1922, at the age of 83, Sarah died in her sleep. She left all of her possession to her niece, Frances Marriot, who had been handling most of Sarah’s business affairs for some time.

Her wealth, by this time, had depleted considerably. The furnishings, personal belongings and surplus construction and decorative materials were removed and the structure was sold to a group of investors to be used as a tourist attraction.

Even the moving men were confused when they started removing the furniture. It was a house where downstairs leads neither to the cellar nor upstairs to the roof. It was often a complete maze to the workman seeking a way out with the furnishings.

Chapter 17

The Cattle Kings

'Their property ran the length of the state'

Miller & Lux purchased starving cattle from the ranchos and moved them to their property with good grass.

Cattle barons Miller and Lux could trail their cattle from the Mexican border to the Oregon border and never leave their own land.

The story of these two cattle kings does take a few twists and turns. It starts with young Heinrich Kreiser, born near the Black Forrest in

This handsome Miller & Lux headquarters building in Los Banos still serves the community well as the site of various government and citizen gatherings.
(Google Images)

Germany. Kreiser immigrated to America, landing in New York.

In New York, he worked in a butcher shop. While there, he met a shoe salesman who had purchased a ticket to California. The salesman wanted to sell the ticket. Kreiser purchased it at a reduced price.

Since the ticket he had purchased was not transferable, young Heinrich Kreiser took the name of the ticket's original owner, Henry Miller, and kept it. He proceeded on to San Francisco by boat.

With only six dollars in his pocket when he arrived in San Francisco, the new Henry Miller took a job in a San Francisco butcher shop making sausages. Wanting to be his own boss, young Miller decided to strike out on his own. He wanted to sell, cut and market the beef he sold, but he also wanted to produce it as well. (Photo courtesy Michael Amabile/Espanas Restaurant)

He headed by horseback to the San Joaquin Valley, where he looked for land on which to raise cattle. There were wide-open spaces there, and the land was within easy trailing distance to the mines of the southern Mother Lode.

As he topped a rise, Miller paused on a slope overlooking the huge valley. Spread out over the distance were droves of cattle, each bearing the Double H brand. The cattle belonged to Henry Hildreth and his brothers.

Miller sought out Hildreth and discussed the cattle business with him. Hildreth was disgusted with the cattle business and wanted to return to the gold mines to strike it rich.

Hildreth offered Miller his 8,835 acres for $1.15 per acre, and his 7,500 head of cattle for $5 each. In addition, Miller would get ownership of the Double H brand.

When Henry Miller returned to San Francisco, he visited Charles Lux, who, too, was interested in cattle. At that time, the two were competitors for the San Francisco beef market.

Miller persuaded Lux that they should pool their resources to form the firm of Miller and Lux. Their first agreement was that they would buy land but never sell any. The first land they purchased was the land owned by Henry Hildreth, which was the San Jon de Santa Rita Rancho.

Prior to the gold rush, cattle were valued only for their hides and tallow. An average price for a full-grown steer was seldom more than four dollars.

With the gold rush, there was an insatiable desire for beef. This turned Spanish black cattle into four-legged nuggets.

Cattle prices rose immediately to this unprecedented demand. Beef cattle were bringing $75 per head in San Francisco. The news that there was a big California market for cattle didn't go unnoticed outside the state. Midwestern and eastern beef coming in from Missouri by entrepreneuring young drovers soon disrupted the market.

By the end of 1853, it is said that 62,000 head of cattle had entered the state over the main immigrant roads, and were pastured in the San Joaquin and Sacramento Valleys awaiting market.

Competition to the beef market developed. Cattle prices were being knocked down by the growth in the sheep industry in California. By 1856, cattle prices had dropped to $16 to $18 per head and many Rancheros found themselves heavily in debt and totally unprepared to pay the staggering interest rates.

Miller and Lux began purchasing starved cattle from the ranchos at $8 per head. These cattle barons had the means and mobility to drive their cattle to the Sierra Nevada, or even to Oregon, where prices remained higher.

The Miller and Lux cattle empire controlled millions of acres in California, Nevada, and Oregon. Their land holdings had a profound effect on the settlement of the San Joaquin Valley.

Miller's pattern for later land purchases was to buy out one heir of a rancho, raise cattle on the land as a tenant in common with the remaining heirs, and eventually buy the others out.

He also loaned money to struggling cattle ranchers. He quickly foreclosed on the loans when cattle sales did not enable the borrowers to pay.

When the Homestead Act was passed, Miller found several ways of circumventing the letter and spirit of the law. He would pay employees of the corporation to file homestead claims under agreement to sell it to him when proved up.

Deed records in Merced County indicate that Miller and Lux were Grantees in 287 instances of land transfers, most in 160-acre homestead blocks, between 1863 and 1887.

Miller and Lux monopolized cattle grazing lands on the west side of the San Joaquin, and employed descendants of the earliest Mexican families on the ranch holdings. Consequently, the western part of the San Joaquin Valley retained its Mexican period lifestyle much longer than other parts of California.

In Monterey County, Miller and Lux owned land in the Peachtree Valley, and in Kern County, they shared the title of the county's largest landowners with the Kern County Land Company. Both parties were responsible for nearly all of the major drainage projects and canal systems of the southern San Joaquin Valley.

The "No-Fence Law" of 1872 changed much of the economic dominance from cattle growing to grain farming. This law essentially repealed the Trespass Act of 1850, which required farmers to fence their crops to protect them from free-ranging cattle.

The repeal of the act required livestock owners to fence in their stock, rather than for the farmer to fence them out. This law stimulated the tremendous increase in barbed wire patents during the 1870s.

Chapter 18

Oil Flows in California

'Oil rush rivals gold in the state'

The first actual oil production west of Pennsylvania occurred in Ventura County without drilling any wells at all. This production was the operation in 1859 of George S. Gilbert, a whale-oil merchant.

Gilbert had first investigated oil seepages near Los Angeles. On property belonging to Major Henry Hancock, Gilbert erected a small pot-still with which he produced semi liquid asphaltum when Hancock drove him off the ranch.

Undaunted, Gilbert then moved north and erected another small still in the canyon of the Ventura River. Although the output was minute and crude by the standards of today, Gilbert's production of kerosene for lighting and of lubricating oil was a genuine pioneer venture. Gilbert's still soon burned down and he became a merchant in Ventura.

The price of crude oil in Pennsylvania rose from $3 to $14 per barrel in less than six months due to

Bellvue No. 1 Blowout
(Google Images)

heavy consumption, causing eastern moguls to look westward for new supplies.

Yale College Professor Benjamin Silliman, Jr., had seen the oil seepages in Ventura County and wrote optimistic reports about their commercial possibilities. His reports didn't go unnoticed by two Pennsylvania companies that wanted to explore California's oil resources.

Thomas A. Scott, of the Pennsylvania Railroad, controlled both firms. The Philadelphia and California Petroleum Company drilled the first oil well in southern California. It was located near Camulos Ranch near Ventura.

They also drilled seven other oil wells in the Ojai region, one of which became the first-known gusher in California. None of the wells in this area were able to sustain themselves.

Wildcatters in the oil business were reminiscent of the gold rush prospectors. When word of a new find went out, everyone rushed to the new site.

By 1884, many companies failed or were absorbed by larger operations. Only four firms were producing oil throughout California at that time.

The Shamrock Gusher, near McKittrick, was California's first truly big gusher. The well there came in at 1,300 barrels per day in 1896. The San Joaquin Valley became the most prolific oil province in California.

In 1898, the "Blue Goose" gusher blew out in the Oil City area of Coalinga in Fresno County.

One of the really big oil well eruptions occurred in Lost Hills, when a wildcat well blew out at a depth of 17,657 feet. It erupted into flame and burned high-pressure condensate gas for 14 days.

No rig personnel were hurt when the well, known as the Bellevue No. 1, blew and erupted into flames in minutes. The hot fire toppled and melted the rig, the mud log trailer, and everything else on the well site.

The flame shot as tall as 300 feet and was visible 40 miles away. Even well control specialists Boots and Coots were unable to extinguish the flames.

The well snuffed the fire out by itself on the 16th day when water began flowing with the gas. An uncontrolled mixture of gas, condensate and water continued to flow for another six months.

Finally, drillers intercepted the well bore of the blowout at 16,600 feet with a deviated relief well, drilled from several hundred yards away.

California Indians Used Oil Seeps

Spanish explorers saw Yokuts Indians using asphalt for a number of purposes in the late 1700s. The Tuolumne Yokuts collected tar from natural seeps that oozed up near their village of Wogitu, near McKittrick, on the west side of the San Joaquin Valley.

The asphalt was molded into fist-sized tar balls for trading, waterproofing, and as an adhesive. The Indians also used the tar for decorating by inlaying bits of abalone shell into tar stuck on pottery, knives, masks and clothes.

In 1864, John Hambleton and Judge Lovejoy dug shallow pits, eight to 10 feet deep, near active seeps in what became known as the "Asphalto" area. They built a small still and refined the tar into lamp kerosene, which was shipped by wagon to their agents in Stockton.

By 1891, several five by six foot shafts, many lined with railroad ties for stability, were sunk up to one hundred feet deep into the McKittrick tar seeps.

Because the miners working these shafts quickly became covered with asphalt, they usually worked naked. At day's end, they cleaned themselves with case knives or wooden scrapers made for racehorses, and then washed with distillate.

Because it was impractical to clean up at noon, they ate lunch "au naturale" sitting on newspapers at the camp mess.

Chapter 19

Stockton Is Major Port

Ben Holt, an inventor of agricultural equipment.

(Google Image)

The San Joaquin Delta is created by the confluence of several rivers and many man-made channels. It is popularly known as "one thousand miles of waterway."

As early as 1856, Stockton was recognized as a major shipping point for California. It's location at the head of a navigable channel, approximately 90 miles inland from San Francisco Bay, enables the city to continue to serve as a major shipping point for many agricultural and manufactured products of Northern California.

As a harbor, in point of capacity, Stockton possesses advantages over all other inland cities of California [in that] there is sufficient depth and breadth of water, at all seasons of the year, for all purposes of moorage and navigation."

German immigrant Charles M. Weber formed the City of Stockton in 1849. He had acquired more than 49,000 acres of land through a Spanish land grant. Unsuccessful at mining for gold, Weber soon realized the true gold lay in providing products for the rush of gold-seekers invading the state.

In its early days, Stockton bore such unpleasant sounding names as "Tuleberg" and "Mudville. But founder Weber elected to name it after Commodore Robert F. Stockton, who gained the nickname of "Fighting Bob."

As commander-in-chief of the Pacific Squadron at the start of the Mexican War, Captain Stockton played an instrumental role in securing the territory of California for the United States. He and his troops marched into Los Angeles on August 13, 1846 and took the city with no opposition.

While unsuccessful in their efforts, attempts were made to name Stockton the state's permanent site for a State Capitol.

Stockton is an inland deep-water port, connected to San Francisco by a 78-mile channel.

It began as a gold town, and was known as the "city of the Thousand Tents."

The city is surrounded by rich peat soils and its temperate climate has combined to make Stockton one of the richest agricultural and dairy regions in all of California. Throughout Stockton's 150-year history, every major fruit, nut, and field crop has been grown there.

Contributing heavily to Stockton's history are the remarkable inventions of Benjamin Holt. Finding that heavy farm equipment bogged down in the loose, pliable peat soils of the San Joaquin Delta, Holt used self-laying tracks instead of wheels on his new tractor invention.
Ben Holt

Holt was an impulsive tinkerer who could spend hours in his shops trying out his latest ideas.

On November 24, 1904, the first successful track-type tractor, the "Caterpillar", crawled across a California wheat field, making history every foot of the way.

The commercial success of the Caterpillar was guaranteed once Holt found a way to power it with a gasoline engine in 1908. The impact of the Caterpillar tractor went far beyond agriculture. In World War I, it fought the mud of the Western front, towing equipment for the Allied military forces, and became the inspiration for the British tank.

The City of Stockton is the seat of San Joaquin County. Located in Stockton are the University of the Pacific (1851), Humphreys College (1896), the San Joaquin County Delta College, a junior college, and variety of cultural groups and several military installations.

The Delta Queen racing in Stockton. It was built in Stockton in 1926. (Google Images)

The Delta Queen raced in the Stockton Channel in the late 1930's. The Delta Queen was manufactured in Stockton in 1926 by the California Transportation Company. A hull, fabricated in Scotland, was used to build the ship, which was the largest steamship on the San Joaquin Delta run between Stockton and San Francisco.

The steamers proved not to be profitable, and the Delta Queen was sold for service on the Mississippi River, and, later, the Ohio River, having traversed the Panama Canal.

Chapter 20

Santa Catalina Island

'Legends about hidden treasures'

Santa Catalina Island

People have lived on Santa Catalina Island for at least 7,000 years. The earlier groups of peoples living on the island lived off the rich resources of Santa Catalina, from abalone and other mollusks, to fish, and marine mammals such as sea lions.

Juan Rodriguez Cabrillo discovered Santa Catalina in 1542. A friar aboard his ship recorded the sighting as follows: "They were at dusk near some Islands, which are about seven leagues from the mainland; and because the wind was becalmed they could not reach them that night."

As the boat neared shore, a large number of Indians emerged from among the bushes yelling and dancing, making signs that seemed to urge the sailors to come ashore.

The Indians laid their bows and arrows on the ground and launched a canoe filled with eight or ten Indians, who rowed out to the ship. The crew invited them to board. The Spaniards gave them some beads and trinkets that indeed pleased them.

The priest noted that Cabrillo had named the islands San Salvador (Santa Catalina) and La Victoria (San Clemente) after the ships. Cabrillo was a Portuguese, but was sailing under the Spanish flag.

For the next sixty years, there is no record of a ship touching at the Island.

In 1602, however, the Viceroy of Spain prepared an expedition to set out from Acapulco under the command of Sebastian Vizcaino. When Vizcaino's ship approached the mountains of Catalina, he was certain he had reached two islands.

From a distance, the bulk of land on the east end appeared separated by the sea from that on the west end of the island. There was no real separation by the sea, but only a low-lying area of land not seen from the distance.

Legends persist that there is buried treasure on the island. The brig *Danube*, out of New York, was wrecked in 1824 on the rocks near San Pedro.

Sam Prentiss and other survivors made their way to the San Gabriel Mission.

Here, Prentiss talked with an old Gabrielino Indian called Turei, alleged to be the chieftain from Catalina Island. The 70-year-old Indian, near death, welcomed Prentiss' friendship.

Before Turei died, he told grand stories of rich treasure buried by the Island Indians beneath a tree on Catalina. He sketched a crude map, which launched the legendary treasure hunt by Sam Prentiss.

Prentiss first returned to the wrecked Danube. He salvaged what material he could and built a small craft to sail to Catalina. In the middle of the channel he was caught in a severe storm.

Everything Prentiss owned was washed overboard. His precious treasure map was buried at the bottom of the sea. Prentiss still was able to get to Santa Catalina, where he built a small cabin overlooking Emerald Bay.

For the next 30 years, legend persists, Prentiss hunted sea otter, and fished and sold firewood from the trees he cut down and dug up on his relentless quest for the mysterious treasure.

He was said to be the first white man to die on Catalina Island.

Before he died, Prentiss shared the secret of the buried treasure with Santos Louis Bouchette, adding another bit of legend to the island's history.

Bouchette was the son of one of the survivors of the shipwrecked brig Danube. When Prentiss shared his story with the young sailor, it stimulated Bouchette much the same as it had Prentiss.

He too began the search, but was luckier, or maybe wilier than Prentiss. In the midst of his treasure hunt, Bouchette stumbled across rich veins of silver, lead and gold. There are some who say Bouchette "salted" the mine to encourage heavy financial backing from outsiders.

Whether it is true or not, the mine was incorporated under the name of Mineral Hills Mines Company. Bouchette operated the mine for some years. He is said to have married a French dance-hall girl during one of his trips to shore.

She was not enchanted living on the deserted island. One day in 1876, Bouchette and his wife were seen loading silver ore and a few provisions onto their sailboat. They were never seen again.

The Islanders living on Santa Catalina often made the trip to the mainland and to other Channel Islands in well-crafted canoes. Because the semi-arid Island offered limited plant resources, the Islanders traded sea products for products they might need.

At the time of first European contact, it is thought the people living on Santa Catalina called their island Pimu and themselves Pimungans (or Pimuvit). They were excellent seamen and paddled their plank canoes skillfully across the sometimes-treacherous channel to trade.

After Spanish colonization, their apparently flourishing population declined drastically of new diseases to which they had little immunity. By the mid-1820s, the few Pimungans left had migrated or moved to the mainland.

Mexican Governor Pio Pico awarded Santa Catalina Island to Thomas Robbins as a land grant in 1846, just four days before the United States invaded California. Robbins was a naturalized Mexican citizen who had been living in California for about 20 years.

Law required that to keep land granted to him, the grantee had to use the land. Robbins established a small rancho on the island, but sold it in 1850 to Jose Maria Covarrubias, just two years after California became a part of the United States as the result of the treaty of Guadeloupe Hidalgo.

Chapter 21

The Heyday of Fishing Industry

'Chinese Had Role in Monterey's Cannery Row'

Chinese fishermen were the first to mine the rich fishing resources of Monterey Bay. Chinese settlers had a decided influence on Monterey's early fishing industry, but were not able to overcome the strong biases against them.

There is little remaining physical evidence of the early Chinese settlements on Monterey Bay. Historical accounts seem to differ, but the one most popular indicates that the area's first Chinese inhabitants set up camp in 1851 on the cove of Point Lobos, a few miles south of Cannery Row.

There were some 500 to 600 Chinese fishermen working the deep waters off Monterey by the year 1853. The site of today's Hopkins Marine Station at the north of Cannery Row was known as China point.

China Point Fish Village

Entire Oriental families worked side by side employing fish traps, gill nets and seines to bring in their bounty. By 1900, some 200 to 800 pounds of fresh catch were sent daily to fishmongers on Clay Street in San Francisco.

The Chinese produced great quantities of dried fish, including abalone meats and shark fins. Some of this product was sent to the gold mines in the Sierra Nevada, but the bulk of it was shipped back to the Chinese immigrants' home province in Canton, China.

According to the Monterey County Historical Society, it was an impressive sight to see the arrival of large, ocean-going Chinese junks with their massive lanteen sails.

"These splendid craft would anchor off China Point, where they would unload Oriental goods for the local Chinese, then load their holds with dried squid—a food staple and fertilizer much sought after in China," wrote Jonathan Kemp for the historical society.

The success of the Chinese fisherman came to put them at odds with the Italian-American fisherman who began working the waters of Monterey Bay in the later 1800s.

The homes in the Chinese settlement at China Point were built virtually on the shoreline and many of the village's stilted shanties literally overhung the rocky shore of the bay. The village's flat-bottomed fishing boats were either beached or tied up at the owner's back door.

Poles and ropes were hung with sun-drying fish, and visitors could smell the village before they could see. The Chinese fishermen also spread the highly aromatic squid out to dry in nearby fields.

Typical of most Chinese settlements, the Joss House (shrine) was a dominant part of the Monterey settlement. The Joss became the site of a daily ritual for the Chinese. It was decorated with ornate carvings and bathed in incense.

The Chinese loved to celebrate. One of the most colorful holidays for the Chinese community was the traditional New Year's celebration. Marked by dragons and street parades, firecrackers and fests, the Chinese New Year was also a time of celebration for the area's non-Oriental communities.

The Chinese became victims of the cultural biases and anti-Chinese laws of the late 1800s. There was also strong competition between Chinese and emigrating European fisherman, particularly Italians.

It was the competition between Chinese and emigrating European fishermen, particularly Italians, which led to the growth of the squid into a major product of Monterey Bay waters.

As the Italian fishing community gained primacy on the Bay and at the dockside, the resourceful Chinese took increasingly to the taking of squid by night fishing, when their operations did not conflict directly with those of the Italian crews.

Fishing at night, the Chinese used torches and pitchwood, burned in wire baskets and hung from the sampans to attract the curious squid to their nets. New laws passed between 1875 and 1900 greatly restricted the ability of Chinese to fish and process or sell their catch.

Local residents sided with the non-Chinese fishermen. Some openly called for the removal of the China Point settlement. The issue was settled in 1906 when a suspicious fire raced through the Chinese quarter, destroying virtually every structure except the Joss House.

Regulation prohibited rebuilding the China Point settlement. While some Chinese fisherman relocated elsewhere, the Chinese presence on Monterey Bay never recovered.

Chapter 22

The Legacy of Claus Spreckels

'He built a dynasty with California sugar'

Claus Spreckels was poorly educ ated and of humble origin, but he left a legacy that will live forever.

He came to San Francisco about 1856, where he opened a grocery store. The store was successful and Claus quickly amassed some investment capital. He then bought an interest in a brewery, another success, and Claus was on his way.

As an experiment, in 1873 he planted sugar beets in Aptos (Santa Cruz County). By 1888, he established the Western Beet Sugar Company in Watsonville. While it was the largest beet sugar factory in the U.S., the sugar had to be sent to San Francisco for refining.

He also founded the Pajaro Valley Railroad to transport sugar beets, and extended the line to Moss Landing.

Klaus Spreckels

This wasn't good enough for Spreckels. In 1897, he began building the Spreckels Sugar Factory near Salinas in Monterey County. The Pajaro Valley Railroad was expanded to serve the new sugar refinery and renamed the Pajaro Valley Consolidated Railroad.

Spreckel's son John later took over managing the Spreckels Empire. He founded the Oceanic Steamship Company in 1881 to import Hawaiian sugar.

In 1887, John Spreckels visited San Diego aboard his yacht *Lurline* to stock up on supplies.

The former Spreckels Sugar Factory near Salinas. It is now closed. (Google Images)

He was so impressed with the real estate boom taking place in the city, he invested in construction of a wharf and coal bunkers at the foot of Broadway (then called D Street).

While the real estate boom ended soon, Spreckel's continued to be infatuated by San Diego. He acquired control of the Coronado Beach Company, the Hotel Del Coronado and Coronado Tent City. He also, in 1892, bought the San Diego street railway ystem, changing it from horsepower to electricity.

Spreckels, for a time, owned the *San Francisco Call* morning newspaper. During the time he was making San Diego investments, he purchased the *San Diego Union* newspaper in 1890 and the *Tribune* in 1901.

John Spreckels moved his family permanently to the San Diego area after the 1906 earthquake. The family moved into a new mansion on Glorietta Boulevard in Coronado.

That structure survives today as the Glorietta Bay Inn. Over the next decade, Spreckels became the wealthiest man in San Diego. He owned all of North Island, the San Diego-Coronado Ferry System, Union-Tribune Publishing Co., San Diego Electric Railway, San Diego & Arizona Railway, and Belmont Park at Mission Beach.

Spreckels built several downtown buildings, including the Union Building, the Spreckels Theatre and office building, the San Diego Hotel and the Golden West Hotel.

He employed thousands of people and at one time paid ten percent of all the property taxes in San Diego County.

"Transportation determines the flow of population," said Spreckels. He continued to expand his streetcar system from the downtown area of San Diego to new areas he was developing at Mission Beach, Pacific Beach, and Normal Heights.

Friends described John Spreckels as always being a joker. One day, when John was still a teenager, his mother and sister Emma became curious when a roll of darning yarn popped out of their basket and rolled out of reach.

The next day, another roll hoped out and the basket tipped over. In the weeks that followed, doors opened and closed, untouched by human hands. Chairs jiggled as people prepared to sit down.

One day, when a rocking horse pranced in the hallway, John's father investigated and found a black thread leading to young John's bedroom. There, he found a multitude of threads led into the closet where he discovered John in his mischief control center.

When his father, Claus Spreckels, broke into laughter, his relieved son joined in.

Out of all the enterprises undertaken by John D. Spreckels, the San Diego-Arizona Railroad was the only one that didn't pan out—not even after it was finally finished.

Back in the mid-1880s, San Diegans felt their city was the logical destination for the first western rail terminus. But northern Californians argued that the gold mines of Sacramento and the bay of San Francisco were a more logical choice.

As efforts to build a railroad in San Diego would begin, something always got in the way. Funds would run out, the tracks would be flooded, and plans would simply fall through, and San Diego shops and other business ventures would suffer and the brief railroad boom turned to bust.

Los Angeles businessmen liked it that way. They would spread rumors, such as, "San Diego is infested with fleas." "It has no water." And, "The city burned down last week."

It was during one of these down cycles that John Spreckels sailed into town. Only 34-years-old at the time, he was an astute businessman and could see San Diego's potential.

Spreckels began buying up failing businesses, including the Hotel Del Coronado, the trolley system, the *San Diego Union,* and the San Diego and Arizona Railroad.

It soon became clear that even Spreckels couldn't do for the railroad what his predecessors had tried and failed. By 1916 the railroad still wasn't finished and 25 percent of it had washed away by the worst flood in San Diego history.

Spreckels sold off some of his investments in order to rebuild the railroad. On November 15, 1919, he finally drove the final golden spike for the completion of the railroad.

The railroad, however, proved too expensive to maintain. The steep grades and scorching deserts soon defeated it. Even its operators changed the initials of the SD&A railroad to mean, "Slow, Dirty and Aggravating." It also became a favorite target of train robbers and banditos.

After John Spreckels death in 1926 at age 72, the Spreckels family sold the line to Southern Pacific for nine cents on the dollar.

Chapter 23

The Russians Arrive

Fort Ross (Google Images)

Nikolai Resanov had arrived at Sitka, Alaska, in 1805 as an inspector and agent for the Russian-American Company. He found the colony there on the verge of starvation and decided to sail southward to Spanish California in search of relief supplies.

When he and his scurvy-stricken crew passed through the Golden Gate, Rezanov knew that foreign ships were forbidden by Spanish rule to trade in California. Still, he boldly sailed his ship, the *Juno*, past the Spanish guns at the mouth of the harbor.

For the next six weeks, the Juno lay at anchor in San Francisco Bay while a battle of wits went on between the Russians and the Spanish. The impasse was broken when Rezanov, who had fallen in love with the commandant's daughter, Concepcion Arguello, proposed to marry the beautiful young lady.

The Juno was soon being loaded with grain for the starving settlement in Alaska, and on May 21, passed out of the Golden Gate.

From that trip, Rezanov resolved to establish permanent trade relations with Spanish California, and he wanted to found a trading post north of the Spanish territory. Rezanov took his plans back to his employer, Alexander Baranov.

The Russians had developed the hunting of sea otter to a very high degree, and taught the natives in Alaska how to kill the animals in greater numbers.

Yankee shipmasters, learning of the sea otter trade, soon became rivals of the Russians for the valuable otters. It wasn't many years before the sea otter population became scarce because of the wanton overkill by both the Russians and the Yankees.

Both the Russians and the Americans looked south to the California coasts. Eventually, the Boston sea captains bargained with the Russians.

A lone sea otter taking the sun.

(Google Images)

The Yankees would furnish mother ships that the Russians lacked, while Gov. Aleksandr Baranov of Alaska agreed to furnish Aleut Indians experienced in hunting otter. The catch would be divided, with no regard that the hunting was to be done in Spanish-California waters.

While the Spanish didn't like this, there was little they could do about it. For one thing, the Spanish had no navy.

Baranov dispatched Ivan Kuskov, an employee of long standing, on a voyage to locate a site suitable for a Russian settlement. Kuskov decided that the most suitable location for a colony was 18 miles to the north at a Kashaya Indian village.

Whether it is true or not, one account says the entire area was acquired from the natives for “three blankets, three pairs of breeches, two axes, three hoes, and some beads.”

The site’s attributes included a small harbor of sorts, plentiful water, good forage, and a nearby supply of wood for the construction of a fort. Perhaps more important, at least in Kuskov’s mind, was the fact it was relatively distant from the Spanish who proved to be unwilling neighbors for the next 29 years.

When the fort was completed in a few weeks, it was named Fort Ross. The name Ross is generally considered to be a shortened version of “Rossiya,” the Russia of Tsarist days. The Spaniard’s San Sebastian River became the Russian River, by which it is still known.

The Russians were very proficient at hunting and killing the fur-bearing sea otters. At one time Fort Ross had a Russian population of some 800 persons, rivaling the largest of the Spanish villages to the south. Their farms, too, were spread over a wide acreage.

When the Russian-American Company decided to abandon the Fort Ross colony about 1839, it tried to sell the property to the Mexican government. When that failed, they approached Mariano Vallejo and others.

In 1841, they reached an agreement with John Sutter, of Sutter’s Fort, in the Sacramento Valley. In a few months, the Russians were gone.

Chapter 24

Joe Walker and Yosemite Valley

Joe Walker

When Joseph Reddeford Walker crossed the Sierra Nevada in 1833, it was through what are now Mono, Mariposa, and Tuolumne counties. While crossing the Sierra Nevada, Walker and his party were the first white men to gaze upon the Yosemite Valley.

"Reliable knowledge of the Sierra Nevada, really begins with this expedition," says one historian.

Walker and his men traveled down the Humboldt River Valley in Nevada and on south by Carson Lake, and then westward across the Sierra. After crossing the summit of the pass, the party became lost for several days in a maze of lakes and mountains.

The description of the region, as given by Zenas Leonard, chronicler of the expedition, accords well with the character of the country in the vicinity of Virginia Canyon.

While moving down between the Tuolumne and Merced rivers, the party saw either the Merced Grove or the Tuolumne Grove of *Sequoia gigantea,* making them the first explorers to see the big redwood trees of the Sierra Nevada.

Walker was born in Tennessee in 1798 and raised on the Missouri frontier. In 1832, he joined a party of 110 hunters and trappers under the command of B.L.E. de Bonneville. Bonneville was a French-born U.S. Army officer who was detached from active service and ordered to lead a military intelligence gathering expedition through the far west.

Captain Bonneville's two most important accomplishments were the leading of wagons through the South Pass and the sending of Walker to spy on the Mexicans in California.

Joe Walker led a detachment of 70 men, including Zenas Leonard, his second-in-command, clerk, and journal keeper. His orders were to find a way to the Pacific through the "unknown country to the west."

Instead of following the route of Jedediah Smith, Walker led his men on a westward route around the shores of the Great Salt Lake. They reached the headwaters of the Humboldt River, then known as "Mary's River.

Walker and his men followed the Humboldt River to its sink, where 800 to 900 hostile Paiute Indians confronted him. When warning shots failed to disperse them, Walker's men fired into them, killing 39 of the braves.

The following year, when Walker made a southerly exit from the Sierra Nevada, his group again accosted hostile Paiutes. Fourteen of them were slain by Walker's muskets.

While historians are unsure of exactly where Walker and his men crested the Sierra, one thing they do know is that the descent from the Sierra crest was more dangerous and difficult than the ascent.

During the descent, Walker lost 24 horses, 17 of which provided nourishment for his famished followers.

Zenas Leonard wrote in his account, "Some of these precipices appeared to us to be more than a mile high. Some of the men thought that if we could succeed in descending one of these precipices to the bottom, we might thus work our way into the valley below, but on making several attempts we found it utterly impossible for a man to descend, to say nothing of our horses."

Walker continued to lead parties throughout the western territory, including serving with

Captain John C. Fremont's exploring expedition to California in 1845-46.

Joseph R. Walker (Google Images)

In that same year, he also drove 500 head of horses from California to Santa Fe.

Joseph Rutherford Walker, fur trapper, hunter, trail blazer, explorer, military guide, cattleman, miner, and sheriff. Capt. Joe Walker was one of the most interesting men that lived during the 1800s.

Hubert Howe Bancroft said, "Captain Joe Walker was one of the bravest and most skilled of the mountain men; none was better acquainted than he with the geography or the native tribes of the Great Basin; and he was withal less boastful and pretentious than most of his class.

"I was strongly impressed by the simple and upright character of Capt. Walker, and his mountain comrades spoke in the highest praise of his ability."

Fremont, Kit Carson, Bill Williams, Alex Godey, Vincenthaler, Ferguson, and others, all agreed in saying that as a mountain man, Captain Walker had no superior." These were the words of Lafayette Bunnell, the man that named Yosemite Valley. Bunnell met with Capt. Walker on numerous occasions in the 1850s to discuss Walker's route over the Sierra Nevada Mountains into the San Joaquin Valley.

Seemingly always on the move, Walker returned to California and engaged in the cattle business in Monterey County in 1851-1858. He and Kit Carson served as guides for $7 per day with Colonel Willison Hoffman down the Colorado

River from Fort Mohave to Fort Yuma, in 1858 and in 1859.

In the spring of 1861, Walker went from Contra Costa County to Kernville, California, where he became Captain of a party organized to rediscover gold on the Little Colorado River.

The party failed to find any gold. Walker returned to California in 1867 to live with his nephew, James T. Walker, in Ygnacio Valley, Contra Costa County. He died October 27, 1876 at the age of 78. He is buried in Alhambra Cemetery at Martinez, California.

Chapter 25

The Story of Ben Raspberry

'Rabbit hunting made him a rich man'

The old-timers around Angels Camp tell this story with glee.

It concerns Bennager Raspberry, a not very prosperous gold miner that tried to eke out a living on a worked-out placer mine.

Raspberry, when he was hungry or just plain had nothing else to do, would kill jackrabbits that abounded around Angels Camp. After shooting several of the jackrabbits one day, the barrel of his gun became jammed with the ramrod.

Try as he might, Raspberry could not break it loose. Exasperated, and in a fit of temper, Raspberry fired the weapon at a rock a dozen feet away. The ramrod did indeed loosen, and when it did, it hit the weathered crust of the rock at which Raspberry had fired.

The Angels Camp Mercantile was originally especial by George Angel, who decided selling to gold miners was better than being one.

The miner couldn't believe his eyes when he saw the rock broken by the ramrod.Gold gleamed from the inside of the broken stone.

Raspberry is said to have gathered $700 worth of nuggets from the area before dark. When daylight arrived, he returned with a pick and a shovel and harvested another $2,000 worth.

The following day, he gleaned even more, netting $7,000 from the vein he had discovered. It was then that he figured he had a gold mine and had better file a claim on the site

Bennager Raspberry is said to have soon become the richest man in town, and his name is perpetuated on an Angels Camp street sign denoting Raspberry Lane.

George Angel, a veteran of the war with Mexico, founded Angels Camp. Angel traveled to the Sierra foothills with a group of gold-hungry ex-soldiers. Angel found a likely spot to camp on the bank of a small creek tributary to the Stanislaus River.

There were throngs of hopeful prospectors working the gravels of the river. Angel decided he would set up a trading post instead of working with a gold pan and a shovel.

As squabbles frequently arose among miners, especially after the easy gold pickings had disappeared, Angels Camp found it necessary to legalize mining claims. Too often a prospector reported "a snake in the tent" when he found a stranger working their favorite location.

Law and order eventually descended on Angels Camp, and a legally appointed sheriff duly arrested most wrong doers. This was not always the case, however.

There is the case of a miner who killed another who had called him a "hog thief." The miner said he had "sort of borrowed" the pig in question, although he admitted he had "et some of it."

Some Angels Camp miners thought the culprit should be strung up pronto. When lynching rumors spread, the sheriff sent to nearby San Andreas for aid in protecting the prisoner, while at the same time rushing trial procedure.

To a packed courtroom came the word that the San Andreas sheriff and emergency posse were nearing Angels Camp.

As if by pre-arrangement, each court officer was seized and bound, and the prisoner was hustled to the hanging tree. When the San Andreas lawmen rode up, the prisoner's body was dangling from the end of a rope.

Today, the tourist knows Angels Camp better than almost any other town in the Mother Lode. Much of this notoriety is unquestionably due to Mark Twain's account of the Jumping Frog of Calaveras County.

Chapter 26

The $40,000 Nugget

'It weighed 195 pounds

(Google Images)

Working 15 feet below ground level, four Americans and one Swiss miner labored their claim at Carson Hill.

As darkness was creeping in on the five prospectors, they kept digging, hoping to find that illusive yellow metal that brought so many to California's foothills.

Suddenly, one of them, generally thought to be a man named Perkins, struck a rock. The rock was heavy, and Perkins was having a difficult time lifting it out of the hole. He decided to take a closer look at it.

What he saw was a big gold nugget. The miners took the nugget to Stockton where it was weighed on the Adams Express Company scales. Newspapers variously reported the weight of the nugget at anywhere from 141 pounds to 214 pounds.

Eventually, its true weight was established at 195 pounds. The miners apparently decided that since Perkins owned the biggest share of the claim, he was also the principal owner of the nugget. The most Perkins had ever realized in his years of prospecting was $200 in gold dust.

The story goes that Perkins and a fellow miner headed for New York with their prize. At some point along the journey, a New Orleans man offered Perkins $40,000 for the nugget, which he accepted, then promptly dropped from history.

The big gold nugget was taken to New Orleans and deposited in the Bank of Louisiana. It was later sold, and the new owner took it to Paris where it was exhibited as the largest nugget ever taken out of California or the United States.

The Gold Rush expended 125 million troy ounces of gold, worth more than $50 billion by today's standards. It is believed that more than 80 percent of the gold in the Mother Lode is still in the ground.

When the name "Mother Lode" was first coined, it referred to only five counties: Mariposa, Tuolumne, Calaveras, Amador and El Dorado. Eventually, however, more gold was taken from Placer, Nevada, Sierra and Plumas counties than was found in the original Mother Lode designates.

At one point, eggs (if they could be found) were $3 each and whiskey was $16 a bottle.

The world's largest gold nugget was the "Welcome Stranger" found in Australia in 1869. It weighed in at 200 pounds. Two men, whose cart got stuck in a muddy road, had to remove a large rock that was in their way. That rock was solid gold.

There were many other lucky finds on Carson Hill. A man named Hance found a 14-pound lump of gold lying at the top of a hill.

The man for whom Carson Hill was named shared little of the wealth produced there. His name was James S. Carson, a sergeant in Colonel J. D. Stevenson's New York Volunteers.

When the regiment was disbanded at the end of the Mexican War, Carson was stranded in Monterey, along with many of the other soldiers. With the news of James Marshall's discovery of gold at Sutter's Mill, Carson joined a company of ninety-two men going to the gold fields.

Other notable names in the party were the Murphy brothers who headed northeast and founded Murphy's Camp, and George Angel, who founded Angels Camp.

While the others scattered to locate claims, Carson was too ill with "rheumatism" or some other affliction that incapacitated him. After many months in bed, he went back to the creek, but became ill again, this time even more seriously, and he was taken to Stockton.

Carson recovered long enough to be elected to the state legislature from Calaveras County. He was making plans to return to his claim when he was stricken with his final illness. He died in Stockton in near poverty in 1853.

Chapter 27

The Big House

'Every man entering San Quentin will have his life changed'

Clinton Duffy

San Quentin Prison is California's oldest and best-known correctional institution. It was established in July 1852 in Marin County as an answer for the rampant lawlessness in California.

It hardly lived up to its supposed purpose, as lawlessness inside the prison continued to be rampant, as well as overlooked by officials. The facility housed both male and female inmates until 1933.

At first, in 1851, a temporary prison was set up on the *Waban,* a 268-ton ship. It quickly

Lawlessness inside San Quinton Prison continued to be rampant. (Google Images)

became overcrowded, escapes were common, and it became difficult to keep prisoners employed at useful work.

On July 14, 1852, this ship was towed to Point San Quentin, arriving at the Point on Bastille Day. Finding work for prisoners often proved difficult. Roadwork and work in quarries was not possible in wet and rainy weather, and on foggy days, prisoners had to be confined to areas that were surrounded by walls.

In 1854, the first cellblock, called "the Stones," was erected. In those days prisoners wore their civilian clothes until they were in tatters. Drunkenness was common inside the prison.

There were 600 prisoners at San Quentin in 1857, many who suffered from respiratory disease. The "Wall" surrounding San Quentin enclosed five acres. Escapes were generally mass escapes of fifty men or more. The local citizenry would come out with deer rifles and help give chase. They also shot to kill.

For the criminal, spending time in San Quentin took on the aura of being decorated for bravery." Chaplain Harry Howard wrote in his book, "Changed Lives at San Quentin." Howard added, "A criminal record that includes time in "Q" was like adding a campaign ribbon to the tunic of a war hero. San Quentin became the graduate school of crime."

In reality, however, Howard said, San Quentin was the proving ground for stupidity. "The inmates made it brutal on themselves. It was as if the prison wasn't as tough as they'd expected, so they adopted a criminal code which allowed them to brutalize each other."

The prisoners established a pecking-order tradition among themselves that was based on violence, perversion and sadomasochism. Once this tradition was started, said Howard, it was almost impossible to stop. Prison officials tolerated it because it created the illusion of peace among the inmates and the measures required to curb it couldn't effectively be executed within existing prison budgets.

Drugs in prison were prevalent. "Young men can sell their bodies for a fix," said

Howard. "They become subject to the authority of the prisoner cult boss. Others may become soldiers to enforce the orders of the cult leaders."

In San Quentin's early years, it was a wild inner society by any measure.

The name San Quentin came from an Indian warrior, Punta de Quentin. He was sub-chief of Chief Marin. Punta de Quentin led the Licatuit Indians in their last stand against the Mexican troops at the spot now occupied by San Quentin. The "San" was added to the Quentin name because at the time, the local population was zealously Catholic.

At first, San Quentin had no bathroom facilities. Buckets of human waste were collected each morning. Neither was there any electricity or heat.

There were frequent beatings of prisoners, as well as solitary confinement in the prison's Dungeon. Maggots often as not were present in the meat supply, and opium use, murders and rape were common.

In its early years, San Quentin used prisoners to construct window sash and blinds and some furniture. Organized labor opposed this as "free" convict labor competing with outside labor.

California, at the time, had a seemingly insatiable demand for burlap bags for wheat, barley, rice and beans. These bags were mostly imported from India and there was no American competition. The prison erected a jute mill, and using raw jute from India, the mill operated on a 24-hour schedule.

Guards at San Quentin received fifty dollars a month and worked ten hours a day, seven days a week. Among the concessions given workers was that meat could be purchased from the prison at wholesale prices. Steaks were about ten cents a pound.

Prison officials dealt with all kinds of characters. There was one prisoner who was a stonemason and had certain skills with cement and stone. He worked alone and was assigned to building artistic walls and borders, generally on the terrace at the warden's residence.

He was released after serving his time. After several months, he was back in prison on another conviction. He asked if he could have his old job back. Officials said there were no tools available for that type of work.

The prisoner said he would take care of that. He went out on the grounds and recovered the tools he had cached away before he left.

Clinton T. Duffy is considered to be the most famous and most humane warden San Quentin ever had. His father before him had been a prison guard, and Duffy was born at San Quentin.

At age 42, Duffy was asked to become warden. His first official act was to fire the Captain of the Yard, a man who encouraged his guards to beat prisoners.

Next, he abolished the Dungeon, a 45-foot cave with no light nor bedding, no water nor other facilities of any kind. The second day of his duties, Duffy outlawed whips, straps, and rubber hoses. He also instructed the cook to start putting dumplings in the gravy.

Writer Sherri Jilek, in her story of San Francisco's "Big House," said Warden Duffy believed a man well fed was a less surly man. "Duffy didn't abolish punishment. He abolished cruelty."

Duffy had fresh water plumbed into the prison for the first time. Previously, salt water had been pumped from San Francisco Bay.

San Quentin, over the years, held the likes of stagecoach robber Black Bart, Tiburcio Vasquez, and cult killer Charles Manson.

San Quentin's days may be at a close. Some state officials say the prison is outdated, unsafe and is falling apart. The fact that it sits on prime development land may be additional reason.

Prison Slanguage

Blow your top: *Lose your cool.*
Bum Beef: *Illegally convicted.*
Caught in a snowstorm: *Drugged with cocaine.*
Crate: *Automobile.*
Coppers: *Credits for good behavior.*
Croaker: *A doctor.*
Dip: *A pickpocket.*
Fish: *A new arrival in prison.*
Eye: *A detective.*
Jury: *Two six-shooters.*
Pete: *A safe.*
Sniff the eggs: *Be executed by gas.*
Tall weed in the grass: *Stool pigeon is listening.*

Chapter 28

Return of the Swallows

'

Mission San Juan Capistrano (Google Images)

The swallows are Capistrano's most famous citizens. They are protected by city ordinance. Anyone destroying a swallow's nest would be severely chastised if not evicted.

Each year, on March 19th, which is St. Joseph's Day, the first band of swallows return from Goya,

Corrientes, Argentina. They make this 7,500-mile trip to and from Argentina where they over-winter.

The swallows confound scientists. During the flight, which lasts for 30 days, the swallows do not eat or drink. They are hell-bent on their destination. They do cleverly fly at altitudes of more than 6,600 feet, taking advantage of favorable tail winds. They also avoid predator birds at that height.

The flight begins in Goya and follows the valleys of the Parana and Paraguay rivers. The swallows do not cross the Andes until they have reached the Gulf of Mexico.

San Juan Capistrano is often called the "Jewel of the Missions." The stone church started as a vision of Padre Junipero Serra. The Juaneno Mission Indians wanted to build the most magnificent structure of all the missions. It is said they wanted to build a church so majestic and so beautiful that even God would be impressed.

Historians believe they may have succeeded. The Great Stone Church, as it came to be called, was a man-made, heaven inspired masterpiece.

All the care and devotion that went into the structure didn't stop the destruction by the earthquake of 1812. Forty of the Indians attending church during that giant tremor were killed. They are still buried in a little cemetery behind the church.

Photo of Mission San Juan Capistrano from the early 1900's.

In his book, *Capistrano Nights,* Father St. John O'Sullivan, Pastor of Mission San Juan Capistrano, 1910-33, relates how the swallows first came to call the mission home.

One day, while walking through town, Fr. O'Sullivan saw a shopkeeper, broomstick in hand, knocking down the conically shaped mud swallow nests that were under the eaves of his shop. The birds were darting back and forth through the air squealing over the destruction of their homes.

"What in the world are you doing?" Fr. O'Sullivan asked.

"Why, these dirty birds are a nuisance and I am getting rid of them!" the shopkeeper responded.

"But where can they go?"

"I don't know and I don't care," he replied, slashing away with his pole. "But they've no business here, destroying my property"

Fr. O'Sullivan then said, "Come on swallows, I'll give you shelter. Come to the Mission. There's room enough there for all."

The very next morning, the padre discovered the swallows busy building their nests outside the newly restored sacristy of Father Serra's Church. Another favorite spot was the ruins of the Great Stone Church, which was once lined with hundreds of swallows' nests.

In 1819, there were more than 31,000 animals, including cattle, sheep, horses, mules, goats and pigs on the livestock rolls of the mission. When the earthquake of 1812 hit, there were 1,361 Indian "neophytes" under the care of the padres.

Some historians claim that these Indian natives were treated like slaves and actually locked indoors at night.

When the missions were privatized in 1833, they were stripped of their land holdings. Mission San Juan Capistrano was sold to Don Juan Forster, who actually lived in part of the mission and stored his trade goods in another part.

This accounted for the structure faring better than most missions, which had wood beams and tiles stolen for use in private homes.

The swallows return to California each year to raise their young. They return to the same nests each year, but if the nest hasn't survived the winter, the birds will often rebuild in the same place.

While the swallows are in California nesting and producing their young, each bird ingests about 1,000 insects daily. Their diet might include flies, spiders, and worms. A single band of swallows destroys, in one campaign, a billion insects. All of this is accomplished without damage to man, his fauna or his flora.

Index